EMBROIDERED GAUZE

The Empress Wu of the T'ang Dynasty

EMBROIDERED GAUZE

portraits of famous Chinese ladies

by

ELOISE TALCOTT HIBBERT

Essay Index Reprint Series

BOOKS FOR LIBRARIES PRESS
FREEPORT, NEW YORK

First Published 1941
Reprinted 1969

STANDARD BOOK NUMBER:
8369-1297-7

LIBRARY OF CONGRESS CATALOG CARD NUMBER:
71-90645

PRINTED IN THE UNITED STATES OF AMERICA

'Dress in the Imperial Middle Kingdom was a matter of Imperial decrees. Clothing was worn in accordance with the seasons. If cold weather lasted into late spring, and it was time for the summer garments—which were of gauze—to be worn, we actually wore gauze, but it was lined with silk and padded with cotton.'

'IMPERIAL INCENSE'
BY PRINCESS DER LING

CONTENTS

ILLUSTRATIONS

CHINESE DYNASTIES

Hsia	2205–1767 B.C.
Shang	1766–1122 B.C.
Chou	1122–255 B.C.
Ch'in	221–206 B.C.
Han	206 B.C.–221 A.D.
Three Kingdoms, etc.	221–589 A.D.
Sui	589–618 A.D.
T'ang	618–907 A.D.
Five Dynasties	907–960 A.D.
Sung	960–1280 A.D.
Yuan	1280–1368 A.D.
Ming	1368–1644 A.D.
Ch'ing or Manchu	1644–1912 A.D.

INTRODUCTION

NO one who has studied the history and literature of the Chinese Empire can fail to be impressed by the women of that nation. For the past four thousand years they have played their part gently and quietly behind the scenes with a modesty that commends itself, but which makes the task of revealing their lives exceedingly difficult. There were so many women of outstanding ability among them whose names are mentioned here and there, and yet, when we attempt to reconstruct their lives, the information available is at best meagre and unsatisfactory.

As a great admirer of Chinese women I have endeavoured to piece together in this book the details of the lives of a few outstanding personages. They have been chosen for two reasons. First, because they belong to different epochs of history, and secondly, because as types they are as diversified as possible. We owe a debt to the Jesuit historians who have left behind them detailed records of the lives of the great Empresses, and on these I have drawn freely. In the case of women of lesser historical importance the information has been taken where it could be found. I have related the facts as they are given in various accounts drawn from the original sources of information, but when two accounts of the same incident have differed, I have used the one which seemed the more reliable.

The name of Confucius is mentioned many times in the following pages, and with intention. Confucianism has been the backbone of Chinese family life, the rock, as it were, on which the home was built. The virtues associated with the teachings of Confucius are practised as a matter of course by the majority of Chinese women, and his sane and reasonable philosophy has been their salvation in times of national emergency and distress.

The summer dress of the ladies of the court at Peking was gauze, as the Princess Der Ling tells us in her book called *Imperial Incense*, but when the weather was cold the gauze garment was wadded with cotton and lined with silk. I have used her words at the beginning of this book because this description seems to me symbolic of the Chinese woman. Her tiny bound feet and dainty clothes appear to preclude her from playing a part in the grim world of necessity, and yet that point of view does not penetrate beneath the surface. Underneath the gauze of the court lady's gown was the warm cotton and serviceable silk, symbolic of the work well done and the solid common sense inherent in the majority of Chinese women.

We are told that the late Empress Dowager of the Manchu dynasty could walk faster and farther than anyone else at her court, even including an occasional European visitor, and yet the high heels of the Manchu lady were placed under the arches of her feet. These women of the Far East may be different from the women of the West, but we have much to learn from them. Patience and endurance are but two of their many virtues, while their strict code of morals could be studied to advantage by the women of today.

It was the mother of Mencius who first stimulated my interest in Chinese women, therefore as not enough is known about her life to devote an entire chapter to her, I think it only right in this introduction to acknowledge my debt of gratitude to a woman who, although she lived more than two thousand years ago, had so much wisdom that we can profit by the lesson of her life. Mencius was a great philosopher and a follower of Confucius. His father died when he was very young and he was brought up by his mother, a woman of remarkable sagacity and foresight. After the death of her husband she settled with her young son in a house near a cemetery, but she very soon realized that she had made a mistake, because the boy at his play imitated the ceremonies of burial which he saw enacted before his eyes. The widow moved to another house near a market, and this time, to her distress, she saw the boy play at buying and selling. However, the mother had learned her lesson. When she moved again it was to a house near a college, and there she had her reward. Her little son was soon busy imitating the learned scholars he saw about him as they applied themselves to their tasks.

Not all the women I have written about were as wise as the mother of Mencius, but as her name was a household word in China until the beginning of the present century, it proves that she symbolized an idea. China was already a great nation, possessed of an ancient culture, when Greece was at the height of her glory. That China is still a great nation while the other civilizations of antiquity have disappeared shows that her women, as well as her men, must possess superior virtues. The wisdom taught by Confucius and practised by the Chinese people has given them strength to retain their independence and to play a part in world affairs during the centuries.

EMBROIDERED GAUZE

I

WIVES, CONCUBINES AND COURTESANS

[48–117 A.D.]

'Sons shall be born to him—
They will be put to sleep on couches;
They will be clothed in robes;
They will have sceptres to play with;
Their cry will be loud.
(Hereafter) they will be resplendent with
    red knee-covers,
The (future) king, the princes of the land.

Daughters shall be born to him—
They will be put to sleep on the ground;
They will be clothed with wrappers;
They will have tiles to play with.
It will be theirs neither to do wrong nor to
    do good.
Only about the liquor and the food will they
    have to think,
And to cause no sorrow to their parents.'

FROM 'THE BOOK OF ODES,'
TRANSLATED BY JAMES LEGGE

I

WIVES, CONCUBINES AND COURTESANS

TWO thousand five hundred years ago Confucius compiled a code of morals which was destined to become the basis of the social life of the Chinese people. In this code the rules governing the position of the individual in his relation to the family and to the state were clearly defined. They were not idealistic rules impossible for the majority of people to follow. On the contrary, they were precise and practical, because they were based on a profound knowledge of human nature. Man being as he is, Confucius did not attempt to change him. He was only concerned with an endeavour to establish the framework of a society within the confines of which each individual could function for the ultimate benefit of himself and of the state.

All the sweeping social changes associated with the name of Confucius naturally did not take place at once. His writings were subjected to various inter-pretations and commentaries during succeeding ages as each dynasty produced scholars who added their own contribution to what had survived of his original words. The Confucian ideals evolved gradually and were adopted with enthusiasm during the reigns of certain rulers and with reservations whenever a reaction against these ideals took place, but they survived with an amazing tenacity, possibly because the system of education of the country was, until the present century, based on the study of the Confucian classics.

The necessity for the strict regulation of family life and the elaborate ceremonies advocated by Confucius and his followers can only be understood if the conditions which existed at the beginnings of Chinese civilization are taken into consideration. For an indeterminate length of time the social customs of the country had been, as a modern writer says, raw and free. The famous Spring and Autumn Festivals were celebrated by both sexes, who apparently had equal rights and equal opportunities for enjoying themselves. Boys and girls sought each other out at these periods of the year and indulged in a series of games which might almost be called orgies of a sexual nature and which seem to have had the significance of a fertility rite. The games are referred to in the following poem:

> 'Beyond the Wei
> The ground is large and fit for pleasure
> So the gentlemen and ladies
> Make sport together,
> Presenting one another with small peonies.'

WIVES, CONCUBINES AND COURTESANS

The same *Book of Odes* contains many poems which indicate that the seclusion of women was unknown in antiquity, and it may have been instituted as a protest against the free and easy morals to which these poems refer.

> '*If you, Sir, think kindly of me,*
> *I will hold up my lower garments and wade*
>   *across the Wei.*
> *If you do not think of me,*
> *Is there no other gentleman (to do so)?*
> *You foolish, foolish fellow!*'

And again *The Book of Odes* says:

> '*I pray you, Mr. Chung,*
> *Do not come leaping over my wall;*
> *Do not break my mulberry trees.*
> *Do I care for them?*
> *But I fear my brothers.*
> *You, O Chung, are to be loved,*
> *But the words of my brothers*
> *Are also to be feared.*'

Obviously a state of affairs which allowed a 'Mr. Chung' to leap over walls and invade the sanctity of the home with so little fear of serious consequences to himself, was not to be tolerated. If Mr. Chung wished to continue to leap, arrangements must be made for him to do so elsewhere. Women must be taught their places, and in future virtuous girls, brought up in the careful seclusion of their own homes, were to be given no opportunity to indulge their fancies other than in the world of their dreams. They might write poems about the peonies, but as for presenting one to a member of the opposite sex at a Spring Festival—that was relegated to the past.

In the ideal state advocated by Confucius, marriage was insisted upon for all, and the chastity of women, required primarily to safeguard the family and secure the legitimacy of the son, assumed, as time went on, the semblance of a religious cult. Even the re-marriage of widows was only tolerated at certain times and under the rule of certain dynasties, while during periods of social reaction, such as that of the Sung when the rigid seclusion of women was insisted upon, the remarriage of widows was considered a moral crime.

The seclusion of women can be readily understood when it is realized that the social philosophy of Confucius was based on the fundamental theory of superiority and inferiority. The king was the head of the state and all men owed him obedience. In the same way the father was the head of the family and unquestioning obedience was required from his womenfolk. The three obediences demanded of a woman were: to obey her father, to obey her husband, and, if left a widow, to obey her son. The woman's world was the home, where she presided over the cooking and spinning and all the manifold activities that went on within the confines of her own sphere. She was taught to cultivate the feminine virtues; to be industrious, quiet, neat, docile, and in every way to make herself acceptable to those whom she was called upon to serve. The man's world lay outside the home where it was neither necessary nor desirable for a woman to intrude.

The wife was chosen by the parents of her future husband and the details of the marriage were arranged by a 'go-between,' a professional match-maker, who visited the families of both the bride and the groom and arranged all the important questions relating to the bride's dowry and other financial settlements which were part of the agreement. The question of love did not arise, nor was it supposed to, for the young people were not permitted to see each other until after the ceremony of marriage had been performed. Unless they had happened to play together as children they were complete strangers to one another. Like the 'River-Merchant's wife' in the poem by Li T'ai-po, most brides could say:

> '*At fourteen I married my Lord you.*
> *I never laughed, being bashful.*
> *Lowering my head, I looked at the wall.*
> *Called to a thousand times, I never looked back.*'

But happy were the brides who could add as the second verse of their nuptial hymn:

'At fifteen I stopped scowling,
I desired my dust to be mingled with yours
Forever and forever and forever.'

After the marriage it was the duty of the young wife to serve her mother-in-law as well as all the other members of her husband's family. The dutiful wife rose early and retired late. Her days were filled with a plenitude of household cares. Her youth was spent in work and bearing children, but in her old age she had her reward. Then she in her turn would be served by the wives of her own sons. Old age in China was attended by compensations lacking in our Western civilization. The position of the mother of a family was, in actual practice, so powerful that even an Emperor did not question the authority of his own mother, as the respect due to parents was superior to that accorded to the ancestors. An old proverb runs: 'It is more meritorious to care properly for one's father and mother who are living than to burn incense to ancestors who are dead.'

To insure that the necessary balance between superiority and inferiority should be maintained, the relationship between husband and wife was made formal in the extreme. No liberties were allowed on either side. Husband and wife were not permitted to hang their garments on the same nail nor to keep them in the same basket. They could not drink from the same cup, nor sleep on the same mat. The husband ate first while his wife served him and afterwards she had her meal with the other women of the household. Their intimate emotional life was regulated with definite precision, and minute instructions were given for the observances which preceded a wife entering her husband's chamber. These varied according to the rank of the husband and the position of the wife in his home, but they included such practices as purification by fasting, washing the garments, rinsing the mouth, binding a sachet of scent in the girdle, and above all, tieing the shoe-strings securely; the latter always being regarded as an outward sign of respect. Only when a man had reached the age of seventy could he be really intimate with his wife provided that she had arrived at the age of fifty. After that period they were no longer kept apart, but could quietly prepare for death in each other's company.

Besides his principal wife, a man was entitled to one or more concubines, or secondary wives, according to his means and his station in life. The concubine was subservient to the first wife, but she too had her definite place in the home and her own duties to perform. In fact, it was considered desirable for a husband to take a concubine if his first wife had failed to provide him with a son, as the ceremonies connected with the worship of the ancestors required that the eldest son should succeed his father as high priest at the family altar. This system of multiple wives accounts for the enormous number of sons left behind them by many of the Emperors. During periods of national wealth and the rise of great houses, dancing-girls were kept in the homes of the rulers and nobles in great numbers, and given the title of concubine, but this was the exception and not the rule, for the number of concubines in a household depended on the wealth and position of the master. In general the concubine was an important member of the house-hold, and her position improved in relation to the number of sons which she bore to her lord. Concu-bines could be chosen without the assistance of a 'go-between,' and while they were generally selected for their virtue and womanly qualities, courtesans and even slave girls could be promoted to this position if their association with the master had endured for a sufficient length of time, or when they were con-sidered worthy of such an honour.

If the first wife did not welcome the addition of another woman to the household there was nothing she could do about it. She might be jealous, but custom required her to share her husband with the newcomer without protest. As for the husband, it was considered a grievous fault if he should neglect one of his wives in favour of another. He had his duties to perform towards all of them, and his first wife was sure of having her share of his attention and receiving the respect that was her due no matter how many strangers he might introduce into the home. The system of concubinage took the place of divorce in old China as it was seldom that a wife was sent back to her own people. It insured a husband for

every woman and gave each one a chance to bear
children. It had many disadvantages but it gave to
each woman a secure position. Her life might be
monotonous, but as a modern Chinese writer so aptly
says: 'In every nation the happiness of women does
not depend on how many social advantages they enjoy
but in the quality of the men they live with.'

A woman engaged in the arduous task of running
a home and bringing numerous children into the
world had very little time to devote to her own
education or to perfecting herself in the arts. In any
case she was not encouraged to pursue her education
beyond a certain point as too much learning was considered dangerous to her virtue. This state of mind is
reflected in an old proverb which asserts that 'The
intellectual woman has no need of virtue.' As virtue
was the quality admired above all others by the
Chinese in their women, the intellectual woman with
a wish to improve her mind was usually obliged to
acquire her knowledge by stealth. While we find
many fine scholars, and even poets and writers among
the women who made the most efficient home-
makers, it was not their function to supply their
husbands with intellectual and emotional companion-
ship. When a man needed a woman to share his
mental life with him or to teach him romantic love,
he took her from among the courtesans.

It was one of the courtesan's functions to entertain
the man's friends for him. The women of his own
family were debarred from male society other than

that of their own relatives, and with the exception
of Buddhist priests, who came and went freely in the
home during the periods of Buddhist ascendancy,
very few men ever crossed the threshold of their
lives. The famous Empress Wu of the T'ang dynasty
was reported to have chosen numerous lovers from
among the ranks of the Buddhist priests; perhaps
because they were the only men with whom she could
be on terms of intimacy without creating too great a
scandal. But no such questions of propriety arose in
the case of the courtesans, who were carefully trained
in the art of entertaining men. The courtesan was
the emancipated woman of ancient China. Men of
intellect sought her company because she was at
home in their society. And what was more, she
carried on the musical and artistic traditions of her
country.

Scholars especially seemed to need the stimulus
supplied by the courtesan, even though as a Korean
writer suggests, 'women are more deadly to scholars
than wild horses.' During the Ming and Manchu
dynasties numerous love affairs flourished near the
Confucian Temple at Nanking, where scholars gathered
together for their examinations. It was considered
quite right and proper that the courtesans should
make their home in the vicinity of the Temple, to be
easily available when scholars wished to celebrate
their successes, or when the presence of a sympathetic
woman was necessary to console them for a failure.
To be seen in the company of a famous courtesan

added to a scholar's reputation, and, on the other hand, the reputation of a courtesan was made through her association with men of intellect and ability.

The rules and regulations governing the relationship between a courtesan and her admirer were carefully established, and the lover knew in advance exactly what proportion of his income he would be called upon to hand over to her. The classics of the Ming dynasty contain many helpful hints as to the correct method of terminating such a liaison, the success of which depended in knowing how and when to bring it to an end. If the affair had lasted for more than three months the lover was expected to support the lady until such a time as he could find someone else to take his place. It was stipulated, however, that the second protector should be the equal in rank and fortune of the first.

Many of the courtesans were highly intellectual women who attained positions of historical importance. Very often they married their lovers and became the most respectable of wives and mothers. As we turn over the pages of Chinese history we find numerous references to the courtesans, or the singsong girls, as modern writers call them. They were often girls born of humble parents who were unable to provide a dowry for their daughters. In other cases the girls themselves were either too beautiful or too gifted to be content with husbands of their own class and therefore chose for themselves a profession which allowed them greater scope for their talents than they would have enjoyed in a marriage contracted in the ordinary formal manner.

In the Han dynasty we find mention of the beautiful Flying Swallow, referred to in the poem by the poet Li T'ai-po.

> *'Pray who in the glorious Han Palaces*
> *Can we compare to our own Emperor's Lady*
> *Save Flying Swallow clad in all freshness*
> *Of her incomparable loveliness?'*

Chao Fei-yen was the Chinese name of this fascinating woman and she was the daughter of a musician who had trained her to be a dancing-girl. Her name suggests the quickness and lightness of her feet. After the death of her father, she and her sister made their way to the capital where the Han Emperor Ch'eng had his court. She was not important enough to be summoned to the Emperor's presence, but one night, when he was prowling about the city in disguise, he saw her dancing and was captivated by her beauty. He happened to be in a mood to seek out a woman whose virtue was less rigid than that of his favourite wife, the learned Pan Chieh-yu, who had made the serious mistake of rebuking him in public, so he sent for the Flying Swallow and made her his concubine.

The highly moral and intellectual atmosphere of the court suffered considerably after the arrival of the new concubine. Pan Chieh-yu retired into oblivion to cultivate her poetic gifts, while the Emperor made merry with his dancer in ways which scandalized the court. In the course of time the Flying Swallow was made Empress Consort and she continued to delight her husband with her beauty and grace as long as he lived. After his death, however, she was forced to take her own life, because she had made so many enemies in the palace that she feared a worse fate.

There seems little in this story to have annoyed Yang Kuei-fei, the famous concubine of the Emperor Ming Huang of the T'ang dynasty, when many hundreds of years later she was compared to the Han dancer by the poet Li T'ai-po, but nevertheless she considered the poem an insult and insisted that the poet be banished from court. Neither lady was what might be called a paragon of virtue, but besides their beauty they had this in common: they were both beloved by Emperors and they both died violent deaths before their time.

The Emperor Ch'eng was not the only monarch of the Han dynasty who succeeded in securing a beautiful woman for his harem. His predecessor, the Emperor Wu, was a man of wide interests. Much of his time was spent in searching for the elixir of life and delving into the sources of other Taoist mysteries, but he did find a moment during his busy life to fall in love with a concubine. It was said of her that her breath was as fragrant as the epidendrum, and that her complexion was so delicate that the Emperor feared lest even the contact with silk would injure it.

Another famous beauty of Han times was Sun Shou,

C

who lived during the second century A.D. The history of the later Han dynasty speaks of her as follows:

'Sun Shou had a good complexion and excelled in making herself fascinating. She made her eyebrows thin and arched, and touched up below her eyes to look as if she had been crying. Her hair was dressed to fall on one side. When she walked or stood she swayed as if weak at the waist. Her mouth she held in a forced but restrained simper. That was why she proved so attractive.'

According to one authority, Han beauties used a great deal of powder and rouge. Rice powder and white lead were applied to their shoulders, neck and hands as well as to the face. Even the eighteenth-century 'patch' was fashionable, but it was painted on with black paint. An even more modern touch was the plucked eyebrows. When completely removed, a thin, blue line was drawn to simulate eyebrows at a higher level. The shape and size of these blue lines varied according to the times and fashion. One variety, highly arched, was known as the pathetic eyebrows.

Sometimes lovely women were used by military leaders to ensnare their rivals. Any woman of outstanding beauty and accommodating morals could become a pawn in the political game of chess. As early as the fifth century B.C., Hsi Shih, a famous beauty, was sent by the king of the Yueh State as tribute to his victorious rival the king of Wu. Hsi Shih was carefully trained in the arts of fascination and seduction before her departure, and it was her mission to corrupt her new master and ruin him through her extravagances.

At a later period of history a famous general also used courtesans and dancing-girls for purposes of military strategy. This general, the brother-in-law of the founder of the T'ang dynasty, was a man with an ingenious mind. At one time he found himself surrounded on a mountain by a Nomad horde and cut off from his main body of troops. There seemed little chance of escape until he conceived the idea of sending dancing-girls to the top of a hill to distract the attention of the enemy. While the Nomads gathered below them to see what was going on, the girls performed curious and questionable posturing dances for their benefit. The Chinese general profited by this diversion and escaped down the far side of the mountain with all his men, and before the enemy knew what had happened the Chinese were attacking them in the rear. There was nothing really new in this idea, because the same ruse had been successfully tried by a lieutenant of the first Emperor of the Han dynasty, only in his case puppets were used instead of living women.

In spite of the seclusion of women and the secondary place which they occupied in the Chinese social system, a woman on several occasions played an important part in the rise or fall of a dynasty. P'an Fei, the favourite concubine of the last Emperor of the Southern Ch'i dynasty, who died in A.D. 501, was known as one of the most destructive women in history. Like the Flying Swallow, P'an Fei was a dancer and she is said to have introduced the practice of foot-binding, although there is little evidence to show that such a custom became a general practice before the time of the Sung dynasty. Yang Kuei-fei and her sisters who lived during the eighth century A.D. still wore socks, which were abandoned when foot-binding came into fashion.

The beautiful concubine P'an Fei held the Emperor in subjection and to please her he indulged in all manner of extravagances. No expense was spared in building a palace which would rival in magnificence anything that had ever preceded it. The walls were plastered with a substance mixed with musk so that each room should be impregnated with fragrance. The designs on the floors were taken from nature and executed by the most celebrated artists of the day, one apartment being paved with golden lilies, each one an exquisite example of the goldsmith's art. On the soles of the tiny shoes of the famous concubine flowers were cut in relief, so that with every step she took the impression of a blossom was left upon the ground.

The Emperor was forced to resort to extreme measures to raise funds for all this splendour and his demands upon his subjects were so severe that they became unbearable. The people wept from despair as they walked along the street. Such a situation could not last and in the end an uprising occurred; the people entered the palace and murdered the Emperor. The commander of the victorious forces wished to save the life of P'an Fei and keep her for himself, but he was advised by his officers to put her to death. She was, they said, just the type of woman to destroy a dynasty.

Nearer to our own times an insignificant slave girl unwittingly helped the Manchus establish their dynasty, and some writers attribute their success to her. The Round Faced Beauty was the name of this girl, who, like so many other women of destiny, was passive and unassuming in the acceptance of her fate. She had served the famous Chinese general Wu San Kuei at a banquet, and when her master saw that her looks had attracted the general's attention she was sent as a present to him. The fiery general fell desperately in love with his new slave. He made her his concubine, and as long as he remained in Peking he could not bear to have her out of his sight.

Unfortunately, the destinies of the lovers were influenced by the unlucky star which hovered over the head of the last Emperor of the Ming dynasty. Wu San Kuei was sent to the frontier to guard the Empire against a possible attack from the Manchu invaders, and the Round Faced Beauty was left in the care of

his father at the capital. During his absence the uprising of the rebel general Li Tzu-ch'eng took place
and a message was sent by the Emperor to Wu San
Kuei ordering him to return to Peking with all
possible speed to guard the city against the rebels.
Wu San Kuei was about to obey when he received a
second message stating that Peking had fallen and that
his father was a prisoner in the hands of the rebels.
The Ming Emperor was dead and future events depended on the use made by Wu San Kuei of his large
army. He had two choices before him. Either he
must join with the rebels and present a united front
to the Manchu invaders, or he must throw in his lot
with the Manchus and with their help destroy the
rebel army.

Wu San Kuei hesitated. His father and all the
women of his family were prisoners of the rebel chief,
and his heart was with his Round Faced Beauty, whose
fate was unknown to him. All his uncertainty and
anguish of heart is evident from his letters to his
father, who had been forced to swear allegiance to
Li Tzu-ch'eng. In the first and second of these letters
he asked anxiously after the health of the Lady Ch'en,
the Round Faced Beauty, but in the third letter his
anxiety had become acute.

'I have your letter of the 20th,' he wrote to his
father, 'and note that you have surrendered to the
new Emperor. Under the circumstances it was
the only thing to do to save our women from the

rebels. But your letter goes on to say that the Lady
Ch'en has left Peking on horseback on her way to
my camp. I have seen and heard nothing of her.
Oh, father! how could you thus recklessly allow a
delicate girl of her age to start out on so perilous
an adventure. I had moved my troops to Shan Hai-
kuan, and was seriously thinking of submitting to
Li Tzu-ch'eng. But this news has seriously upset
me.'

Wu San Kuei was even more upset when he learned
that his Lady Ch'en was back in Peking and had been
given to the Ming Heir Apparent as a concubine. He
wrote immediately to the rebel general, who had proclaimed himself Emperor, demanding the surrender
of the Heir Apparent as well as of the Lady Ch'en.
Li Tzu-ch'eng replied as follows:

'The Heir Apparent is safely ensconced in the
Palace so you may abandon all hope of using him
for the furtherance of your schemes. We have
given him a princedom, and we have made over to
him your wife and women for him to dally with as
he pleases.'

This was a direct insult and Wu San Kuei no longer
hesitated. He offered to place himself and his large
army at the service of the Manchus and instead of
opposing the invaders he joined with them on their
march to Peking. The rebel Emperor Li Tzu-ch'eng

was totally defeated and in an attempt to make better terms for himself the Round Faced Beauty was restored to her lord.

Wu San Kuei received as the reward of his services the command of two distant provinces of the Empire, where, far removed from the court, he lived in regal splendour. He built for himself a fine palace, but he did not share it with his Round Faced Beauty. Instead of joining him she chose to enter a Buddhist nunnery and become a nun. Such a decision was not an unusual one. Many of these famous courtesans were at heart simple, virtuous women who preferred death or seclusion rather than to return to the man they loved when their bodies had been—in their own eyes, at least—defiled. The Round Faced Beauty chose a nunnery, in the same spirit as the beautiful Hsi Shih two thousand years earlier had chosen to drown herself when her mission of destruction was accomplished.

The stories of the famous courtesans are more spectacular than those of the wives and mothers of the country who remained faithful to the strict Confucian training of their youth. But the path of virtue was no easy one and the patience with which the secluded women endured their lot has been the inspiration of countless poems as well as of many novels written during the Ming dynasty. From behind the curtained window of her Sedan-chair when she went abroad, many a wife and mother gazed wistfully at the world from which she was debarred. Did she envy those other women, the courtesans, who played and loved and lost, but who, for a brief interval, tasted life to the full and were always willing to pay the price? Even the Master said: 'Rare are they who prefer virtue to the pleasures of sex.'

The King of Wu combing the hair of the beautiful Hsi Shih

II

THE MOST BEAUTIFUL OF CHINESE WOMEN: HSI SHIH

(ABOUT 495–472 B.C.)

'Her fingers were like the blades of the young white grass,
Her skin was like congealed ointment,
Her neck was like the tree grub,
Her teeth were like melon-seeds;
Her forehead cicada-like, her eyebrows like
  (the antennae of the silkworm moth);
What dimples as she artfully smiled!
How lovely her eyes, with the black and white so well
  defined!'

FROM 'THE BOOK OF ODES,'
TRANSLATED BY JAMES LEGGE

Characters in the Story

FU CHAI	*King of Wu*
KOU CHIEN	*King of Yueh*
PO P'I	*Prime Minister of Wu*
WEN CHUNG	*Prime Minister of Yueh*
FAN LI	*Commander of the army of Yueh*
HSI SHIH	*The most beautiful of Chinese women*
CHENG TAN	*Her friend and companion*

II

THE MOST BEAUTIFUL OF CHINESE WOMEN

AGAINST a dark background of political unrest, the figure of Hsi Shih stands out as a symbol of beauty in the midst of strife and disaster. She lived during the fifth century B.C., when the power of the ruling Chou dynasty was in its decline and retained only a shadow of its former greatness and authority. The real rulers of the country were the princes, or kings as they called themselves, of the semi-independent feudal states. Each king had his own court, where he lived in regal style, and his own army with which from time to time he would attack one or more of his neighbours in order to extract tribute from them or to incorporate their lands within the confines of his own.

This period of Chinese history, which is known as that of the Contending States, corresponds in certain respects to the Middle Ages in Europe, when feudalism divided the different countries of the West into small, bellicose principalities. Just as the Middle Ages had their wandering scholars who travelled from court to court, so China during the period of the

Contending States had its philosophers and men of letters who journeyed here and there about the country seeking employment or searching for fertile pastures in which to plant the seeds of their wisdom. Many of these men were of the highest integrity, and their learning and importance were such that they exercised great influence at the courts of the feudal nobles. The wise king or prince was the one who procured the services of the cleverest adviser. At the court of the king of Yueh, where our story opens, King Kou Chien had opened his doors to such men as these, and we shall learn how he profited by their advice.

King Kou Chien was sadly in need of good counsel. He had recently been defeated by his rival, the king of the state of Wu, and for three years he had been kept a prisoner in the latter's capital, which is now known as the city of Soochow. During that time he had been forced to work as a groom in his enemy's stables, and the hardships and humiliations he then endured had filled his heart with bitterness. Fortunately, he had able ministers who schemed for his release, and in the end he was allowed to return to his own home on condition that a large yearly tribute should be sent to the king of Wu. Such clemency was unusual at this period of history, and it was not appreciated by the vanquished ruler of Yueh. On the contrary, he vowed to be revenged. After his return home he slept on brushwood and tasted gall every day to remind himself of the years he had spent as a

prisoner and of his vow to regain the independence
of his native state. Every possible economy was
practised in order to raise funds to build up a powerful army in secret, as no news of his preparations for
war must reach the ears of his enemy. His subjects
were even compelled to marry in order that future
soldiers should be born. Time was no consideration
in ancient China, and for twenty years quiet preparations went on until he had at his disposal a sufficiently
large army to threaten the security of the state of Wu.

King Kou Chien was clever enough to realize that
arms alone would not achieve victory. For that reason
he welcomed to his court all those men whom he
thought would be best able to help him. His prime
minister, Wen Chung, and the commander of his
army, Fan Li, were both men of subtle intellect,
capable of conceiving and executing cunning plans.
As the king knew what he wanted and worked with
only one end in view, circumstances conspired to aid
him. His enemy, Fu Chai, the king of Wu, grew
careless. Frugality disappeared from his court and he
lived a life of ease and extravagance, because the
yearly tribute he received made him rich. He neglected his army and he feared no man now that the
enemy state of Yueh had been rendered impotent. To
make matters worse for him, his prime minister was
a rogue in the pay of his enemies, and all that went
on in the state of Wu was known at the court of
Yueh.

When the clever prime minister of Yueh, Wen

Chung, learned that corruption had already set in at the enemy court, he asked for an audience with his king and suggested the following plan. The king of Wu, he said, might be persuaded to accept the present of a beautiful and accomplished woman as part of the yearly tribute from the state of Yueh. Such a woman, if she had been properly trained, would be able to secure the affections of the king, and once in possession of his heart she would find ways and means to divert his attention from state affairs. A clever woman might even be able to sow seeds of dissension throughout the land once her influence over its ruler had become paramount.

'For,' continued Wen Chung, 'beautiful women have ever been the inspiration of great men and the ruin of others. Their seductive arts of fascination may exercise boundless influence over the most powerful of men and monarchs. In fact, the intangible power of woman's beauty may lead to the salvation or destruction of a nation.'

There was nothing new in the idea of using a woman to ensnare an enemy, and King Kou Chien of Yueh was not showing unusual intelligence when he grasped the possibilities of the scheme and eagerly gave his consent. The difficulty was, of course, to find a woman sufficiently fascinating to appeal to the fancy of a jaded epicure like the king of Wu. Not only beauty was required, but intelligence as well, as only a clever woman would be able to profit by the severe training which would be necessary to fit her for her task. After giving the matter serious consideration, the king of Yueh summoned to his presence the commander of his army, Fan Li, and ordered him to find a supremely beautiful woman who possessed all the desired qualifications.

Drilling an army in secret was one thing, but an intensive search for a beautiful girl was another; Fan Li, however, realized that both tasks were alike in this respect, they both required patience and perseverance. Disguised as a travelling merchant, he trudged from one hamlet to another, often discouraged but never despairing, for, as he said to himself:

'In a hamlet of ten households there must be one honest person; within a space of ten feet there must be a fragrant plant.'

This being the case there was always the possibility of finding rare loveliness within the confines of a small village.

Late one afternoon, when the tired traveller was approaching the hamlet of Chu-lu, he saw a girl kneeling on the stones beside a little stream which flowed through the village, washing silk. He stopped in amazement. Never had he seen such a wonderful woman. As she bent over her work, her attention concentrated on the silks before her, every gesture was harmonious, every movement the poetry of motion. The minister was charmed. Who was this woman? He did not yet know that he was gazing at Hsi Shih, of whom it was later said:

> 'So beautiful was she that the moon hid her face in envy and the flowers blushed for shame at sight of her.'

Fan Li forgot his fatigue as he admired the picture before him, and in his astonishment he said to himself:

> 'Ah, now I am forced to believe that in the retreat of high mountains things unusual are some-tims encountered. My rare discovery here in this little frequented spot is an example. Never before have my eyes feasted on such a creature whose exquisite features would challenge all the maidens of the world and whose alluring smile would indeed overthrow a kingdom.'

The minister stood and watched her until she placed her silks in a basket and started for home. Then he tore himself away from the magic spot and went to make discreet inquiries in the little town. He felt that he had reached the end of his journey, and his heart rejoiced at the success of his quest.

Hsi Shih was the daughter of humble parents. Her father made a precarious living by gathering firewood in the forest and selling it to his neighbours, while her mother was a weaver in the home. Hsi Shih, as a dutiful daughter, helped her parents by washing silk, although she was known throughout the countryside for her extraordinary beauty. Food was scarce and times were hard, and when Hsi Shih was tired or worried she had a habit of knitting her brows which was considered by one ugly woman of her village as being especially attractive. The chroniclers relate that:

> 'This woman, seeing how beautiful Hsi Shih looked, went home, and having worked herself into a fit state of mind, knitted her brows. The result was that the rich people barred their doors and would not come out, while the poor people took their wives and children and departed elsewhere.'

Thus, even within the confines of her own small village, the beauty of Hsi Shih had influenced the lives of others.

Hsi Shih had been well aware that the eyes of a stranger had been turned in her direction as she bent over her work. She was not unaccustomed to admiration. She knew that she was beautiful, and, as she gazed at her own reflection in the clear stream of running water, she thought that such a gift as hers should bring in its train another and a better form of life. She dreamt of the court where she could hold her own amongst the fairest of the land, but the court was a hundred miles away and belonged to a different world. What chance was there for her, dressed as she was in simple clothes, and tied to the work which provided her parents with bread?

Conscious as she had been of the stranger's interest, Hsi Shih was not altogether surprised when the next morning he appeared at the door of her parents' cottage. A visit from an unknown person was an event and there was some consternation in the family until Fan Li revealed his mission. He talked to the father as one patriot to another. Hsi Shih would have the glory of serving her country, and her parents would receive wealth and power in return for their consent. It was agreed between the two men that the girl should be taken to the court and there trained for her future position.

Hsi Shih went gladly. She was to be sacrificed for her country and she knew it, but nevertheless the rôle which she was called upon to play was a tangible one which she could understand. This was not a useless sacrifice, nor were prayers or fasting necessary to prepare her for it. Rather was she to receive the best that the court of a Chinese ruler twenty-five hundred years ago had to offer in the way of education and luxury. Bright years of opportunity were before her, and as an additional reward she would have the esteem and gratitude of her countrymen. Turning to her parents she said:

'My beloved parents, I believe this is the decree of Heaven. If his Excellency thinks that a humble girl like myself may some day render service for the liberation of our nation, I am willing to respond to such a call.'

Then she gathered together her simple possessions and followed the commander of the king's forces. The village was destined to see her no more. Writing a thousand years later, Lou Ying, the poet, says:

> '*When Hsi Shih steeped her yarn*
> *Beside the purling brook,*
> *Like mosses on her washing stone*
> *Men's hearts with yearning shook.*
> *But since she went to Ku Su*
> *And thence returned no more,*
> *For whom do Peach and Plum trees bloom*
> *Along the vernal shore?*'

When Fan Li, accompanied by his charming companion, arrived at the capital, the king was overjoyed and warmly congratulated the minister on the success of his quest. Hsi Shih was installed in suitable apartments, and after a few days of preparation and rest was presented to the king. Kou Chien was too much occupied with his plans for revenge to be susceptible to female charms, but he agreed with Fan Li that the beauty of the girl was without a flaw. He suggested, however, that it would be desirable to have more than one woman to train for such a delicate mission. Fan Li disagreed with him and answered as follows:

'Sire, of pretty maidens there are plenty but there can only be one Hsi Shih, for in the whole state of Yueh her unique combination of beauty, grace and charm stands unequalled.'

The commander of the king's army, although he despaired of finding another girl to train for the same task as the one for which Hsi Shih was destined, realized with the instinctive knowledge of a wise man that young girls must have companions of their own age and station in life, so he sent back to the village for a girl who had been the playmate since childhood of Hsi Shih. The two girls lived together and shared their studies, but all the court realized that Fan Li was right when he said that there was only one Hsi Shih. The companion was called Cheng Tan; she was a quiet, studious girl, content to remain in the background as the shadow and slave of her brilliant friend.

Hsi Shih throve on court life. She enjoyed luxury in every form and everything was new and delightful to her. The two girls spent their days in study. They had tutors to instruct them in the classics and history, as well as calligraphy, singing, and dancing. Their deportment was considered the most important side of their education and they were trained to dress themselves in court robes and observe the rules of palace etiquette. This was before the time when Tartar dress with its short coats and yellow leather boots was introduced, and the long flowing robes in fashion at the time of Hsi Shih required stately and dignified movements. When Hsi Shih walked she swayed with natural grace, and the poets have compared her movements to 'a willow in the breeze.'

Fan Li, the scholar-general who had brought Hsi Shih to court, watched over the progress of his protégée with ever increasing devotion. Was she not in a way a branch of his army, as necessary to his plan of attack as a whole regiment of men? It was his pleasant duty to teach her the art of fascination and all the different ways of capturing the heart of man. This was a dangerous pastime for both pupil and teacher, and Fan Li soon found himself looking into the lovely eyes of Hsi Shih with more interest than was strictly in accordance with his duties. Hsi Shih, on her side, found her heart ready for love, and her natural coquetry made her anxious to practise her newly acquired knowledge on her handsome instructor. As summer took the place of winter, and the moon, that ever kindly friend of lovers, shone brightly on the palace garden, Hsi Shih and her instructor would sit together in the warm dusk and sing to each other of their undying passion. It says much for Fan Li's patriotism that his infatuation for Hsi Shih never went beyond the bounds of song, and as the girl was constantly reminded of her duty to her country by her friend Cheng Tan, she restrained her sentiments in accordance to the dictates of convention. But the love which these two had for each other was imprinted on both their hearts, never to be effaced.

Pleasing a beloved teacher would provide additional stimulus for any woman intent on preparing herself for a great task, and in the circumstances Hsi Shih made rapid progress with her studies. At the end of three years both the king and Fan Li were satisfied that she would be able to fulfil her mission. A delegation was therefore dispatched to the king of Wu requesting his acceptance of two beautiful maidens as part of the yearly tribute from the state of Yueh. Fu Chai, the king of Wu, was flattered. His prime minister, Po P'i, who for many years had been in the pay of the enemy, urged his acceptance of the gift, and only one old minister, a patriot who had served the king's father, ventured to protest.

'I entreat you, Sire,' he said, 'not to fall into the trap that has been laid before you. The king of Yueh would not present such priceless gifts as these without some ulterior motive. Please be wary, for since the dawn of history men have ever been slaves to beautiful women. By accepting these beguiling creatures from our fallen enemy much trouble will surely befall the royal house, leading perhaps to the disintegration of our beloved state.'

But even with apt quotations from historical precedents to confirm his theory, the minister could not convince the king. Fu Chai expressed his pleasure with the gift and his desire that the girls should be sent to him as soon as possible. The delegation

returned to Yueh filled with elation at the success of
its mission.

When the news reached the court of the king of
Yueh that the enemy was prepared to accept the gift,
all was bustle and confusion. Hsi Shih and her companion were dressed in their best with their hair
arranged in the cloud-cluster fashion. No money was
spared on the preparations for their departure. The
girls were equipped like princesses and chariots and
carts were made ready to carry their clothing and
presents for the king of Wu.

It must not be thought, however, that King Kou
Chien of Yueh had forgotten his habits of frugality.
Years of rigid economy had taught him the value of
saving, and he devised an ingenious means of repaying
himself for the money he had spent on the girls. Every
day before their departure Hsi Shih and her companion sat side by side on the tall Phoenix tower
while the people of the state filed by, two by two, to
look at them. A piece of gold was demanded from
each one who availed himself of the privilege of ad-
miring so much beauty, and in this way at least one
branch of the king's arms became self-supporting.

The greater part of the long journey to the capital
of the state of Wu was made by boat, and the girls
amused themselves on the way by playing the guitar
or composing verses. Fan Li accompanied the party,
but it was not in accordance with custom for him to
spend much time in the company of Hsi Shih. He
could watch her from a distance and find what con-

solation he could in the knowledge that she was now an object of national interest, and that he, as her guardian, occupied an honoured position in the eyes of his countrymen.

In the state of Wu great preparations had been made for the reception of the two beauties. The king received them in audience surrounded by his ministers and all his court. As they approached him the jade pendants attached to their girdles made a musical sound and the air was fragrant with the scent of their gowns. Pearl ornaments and kingfisher feathers adorned their hair; the same ornaments which were to be used more than a thousand years later by another beauty, Yang Kuei-fei. Hsi Shih, like Yang Kuei-fei, the beloved of the T'ang Emperor, Ming Huang, became the inspiration of many poets, who told her story over and over again. Tu Fu, who sang so often about his beautiful contemporary, Yang Kuei-fei, looked into the far distant past when he wrote these lines with his brush:

> 'As beauty is of all the world admired,
> Obscurity no longer her could hide.
> That morn a maiden washing by the brook:
> That eve a Prince's bride.
> In humble state how different from the rest?
> When fortune came they noted her, how rare.
> Attendants then she had to tie her hair.
> And aiding hands arranged her silken vest.
> Her Lord's love sought to aid her beauty fair.'

Fu Chai, the king of Wu, looked into the lovely eyes of Hsi Shih and forgot his people and his state. Now she did not turn away and blush as she had done three years previously beside the little brook. She was complete mistress of the art of seduction and she knew how to encourage the king to look again. Fu Chai hardly noticed the second girl, whose quiet charms did not attract him. He had eyes only for Hsi Shih, and before the audience was over those at court realized that the girl would be a force to be reckoned with and that she would be able to influence the king either for good or ill.

The king commanded that the girls be sent to the Pavilion of the Golden Phoenix to await his pleasure. Wine and choice food were served to all his guests, and for the next few days the king and all the court celebrated. The festivities were on a scale hitherto unknown in the history of Wu, and as the poet says:

> *'Behind the hills appears the flush of dawn,*
> *Beyond the river sinks the moon forlorn;*
> *And now the sun climbs up the towers of Su;*
> *What of the revellers in the Halls of Wu?'*

Amidst the revellers in the halls of Wu, Hsi Shih wove her net of fascination about the heart of the susceptible monarch and it was not long before he counted every moment spent away from her side as a moment wasted. She had been an apt pupil, and every device which she had learned from her instructor Fan Li was used for the benefit of the king.

> '*Inflamed by wine, she now begins to sing*
> *The songs of Wu to please the fatuous king;*
> *And in the dance of Tsu she subtly blends*
> *All rhythmic movements to her sensuous ends.*'

All the poets spoke of her drinking and her dancing. Twelve hundred years later Li T'ai-po was to write:

> '*Hsi Shih, the Queen, flushed with wine, dances—*
> *She is fair and unresisting.*
> *Now smiling, she leans near the east window*
> *Against a couch of white jade.*'

But she could do more than sing and dance to amuse the king. She had wit, and her grasp of politics astonished him. When there was anything she wanted she could shed tears which so moved her lover's heart that he could refuse her nothing. For she was, as Fan Li had said, the one and only, the incomparable Hsi Shih, whose magnetic personality attracted everyone, many even against their own will. Soon she became the power behind the throne and there was no one, from the highest to the lowest, in the land who did not strive to gain her favour.

But even as the mistress of a palace and the beloved of a king, Hsi Shih never forgot her mission. She had three methods which she used to influence the king to his disadvantage. The first was to praise his prime minister, the rogue Po P'i, and urge the acceptance of all his suggestions. The second was to destroy the influence of the honest minister who had warned the king against accepting a present of women from an enemy state. And the third was to flatter her lover and encourage him to believe that his own judgment was infallible. It was a subtle plan, worked out in advance by the clever brain of Fan Li, who, when he found that everything was proceeding according to his desire, returned to his own country to make a report to the king of Yueh.

Hsi Shih proved to be a capricious favourite. She wanted new scenes and new amusements all the time. It was part of her plan to lure the king away from his capital to a place sufficiently remote so that communication with his ministers would be rendered difficult. In this way the government would be left in the hands of the prime minister, who had been bribed to work against his master. With this end in view she persuaded her royal lover to build her a palace some thirty li from the capital. The following spring it was completed and was called the Palace of Beautiful Women. Situated in a park ten square miles in area, this palace contained everything that the heart of the most exacting woman could desire. Embroidered silk curtains encrusted with coral and gems, scented furniture and screens inlaid with jade and mother-of-pearl were among the luxuries which surrounded the favourite, while the blinds of her windows were made of real pearls strung on silk threads. And even a lake fringed with willow-trees and crossed by marble bridges was constructed to satisfy her whim of the moment.

On one of the hills near the palace there was a celebrated pool of clear water which has been known ever since as the pool of the king of Wu. Here, to amuse her lover, Hsi Shih would make her toilet, using the pool as a mirror while the infatuated king combed her hair. Other pastoral delights included fishing, and a huge coral bowl was made to hold the goldfish caught by Hsi Shih in the lake. If she played with a bird, a cage was made encrusted with jewels to hold this fortunate object of her favour. Her slightest desire was gratified, to the consternation of the people who realized that her extravagances were emptying the treasury. Messages reached the king at his summer palace urging him to return to the capital and to resume once more the control of the government, but acting on the advice of Hsi Shih, he sent word to his prime minister to arrange matters as best he could.

In reply to an urgent plea for economy the king ordered the construction of a long colonnade on land adjoining the palace. The floor was of white marble, and it was built on top of thousands of earthenware jars so that a hollow cavity was formed, and feet dancing on the terrace resounded like the chiming of bells. Hsi Shih had special shoes made for dancing on the Colonnade of Musical Shoes, as it was called.

Having begun to build palaces to please his beloved, the king did not know when to stop. The royal park was soon filled with pleasure pavilions and halls for music, and additional land was incorporated within the confines of the park so that Hsi Shih, who loved nature and the creatures of the wood, could have the pleasure of watching deer and pheasants. At another time he enlarged a small stream so that she could go on boating excursions. At distances of a hundred feet white marble pavilions for dancing were erected. Brightly dressed girls in groups of ten could be seen posturing in each pavilion as the royal barge passed by.

By the time that two-thirds of the entire revenue of the state had been spent on the caprices of Hsi Shih the situation became desperate, and the king could no longer neglect the repeated requests of his ministers to return to his capital. To prepare for his return a canal was cut through the heart of the city, which added to the general discontent, as houses were torn down to make way for it and farmers were conscripted to work on it when they could least afford to leave their crops. The resentment of the people rose at this new manifestation of their ruler's extravagance.

When things had gone from bad to worse in the state of Wu, Hsi Shih thought that the time had arrived to strike the final blow. So she sent a secret letter to her old admirer, Fan Li, stating that the time seemed propitious for an invasion of Wu. King Fu Chai, she wrote, was getting old, and his army was disorganized. Should he die and his son take his place, wrongs might be righted and the moment of weakness might pass before anything was accomplished. With a new ruler the state of Wu might once more become powerful, and in that case her mission would have failed.

Fan Li communicated this excellent advice to the king of Yueh, who agreed to an immediate attack. Shortly afterwards the state of Wu was invaded by an army of fifty thousand men, led by the king and Fan Li, the commander of his army. Little resistance was offered to stop their advance and the victorious army of Yueh swept through the state until it reached the capital itself. When the outer buildings of the palace went up in flames the king of Wu realized that all was lost; in his extremity he sent a message to his rival begging for mercy and reminding him that many years before he had spared his life. King Kou Chien was inclined to grant his request, but Fan Li, who could not forget that he was dealing with the man who had been the lover of Hsi Shih, remonstrated with him, saying:

> 'When Heaven gave the Prince of Wu the great opportunity of gaining power he did not take advantage of it, and so he is a fugitive today. Should you fail to accept the fortune it has now given you, you too may be driven from your state, and then all the twenty years of hardship that you and your wife have borne will have been endured in vain.'

This reasoning convinced King Kou Chien that clemency was unwise and he refused the request. When the king of Wu learned that he had no hope of mercy, he committed suicide. It is said that his family fled to Japan and became the founders of the present Japanese dynasty.

Fan Li had taken care to have Hsi Shih removed to a place of safety when his soldiers invaded the palace and she was also kept in ignorance of the death of the king. In her place of hiding she received a letter from Fan Li asking her to come to him as his wife. Although the devotion of Hsi Shih for her former instructor had never wavered, she answered that she was unworthy to 'wait upon him with the towel and comb,' and that she preferred to take her own life rather than hurt the reputation of one whose fair name should be handed down to posterity without blemish. She asked for a last interview with her former lover, the king of Wu, stating that she wished to thank him for all his kindness to her.

Fan Li was afraid that Hsi Shih would carry out her threat to take her own life, so a boat was hastily sent for her on the pretext that her request for an interview with the king would be granted. During the journey Hsi Shih learned that her lover was dead. She did not hesitate. Turning to the messenger who was accompanying her, she said:

'Go! Tell your Master that in expiation of this tragedy, I must now bid him a last and fond fare-

well. I prefer to follow the late king of Wu so
that future generations may know that, although I
avenged my country, I was not unmindful of his
Majesty's love and trust. By my action I shall have
faithfully discharged my duty to my country and at
the same time offered atonement for my sin.'

With these words the beautiful Hsi Shih plunged
into the swift current of the river and disappeared.

So died Hsi Shih as many other Chinese women
have died, rather than face dishonour or bring dishonour to the one they love. Her mission was accomplished and her work was done. Of her palace, with
its gardens and pavilions where she had reigned as
queen:

> 'Nothing remains but the moon above the river—
> The moon that once shone on the fair faces
> That smiled in the King's Palace of Wu.'

III

A DESPOTIC EMPRESS: LU HOU

[DIED 181 B.C.]

'A clever man builds a city,
A clever woman lays one low ;
With all her qualifications, that clever woman
Is but an ill-omened bird.
A woman with a long tongue
Is a flight of steps leading to calamity ;
For disorder does not come from heaven,
But is brought about by women.
Among those who cannot be trained or taught
Are women and eunuchs.'

FROM 'THE BOOK OF ODES,'
TRANSLATED BY H. A. GILES

Characters in the Story

SHIH HUANG TI — *The First Supreme Divine Ruler (259–210 B.C.)*

LIU PANG — *His successor. Afterward called Kao Ti, first Emperor of the House of Han*

LU HOU — *His wife. The first Empress of the Han Dynasty*

HUI TI — *Her son. Second Emperor of the Han Dynasty*

THE LADY CH'I — *Favourite concubine of Liu Pang*

JOU-I — *Her son*

HSIANG-CHI — *A rival general*

LIOU-TCHANG — *A Marquis of the House of Han*

III

A DESPOTIC EMPRESS

IN the third century B.C., after a long period of dis-integration during which the great Chou Empire had slowly broken up, the Feudal states that constituted the Chinese world were united under the firm rule of a man who corresponded to what we, in modern times, would call a dictator. To be sure, he styled himself Emperor, or Shih Huang Ti, meaning the First Supreme and Divine Ruler, but he was a dictator all the same, with the good and the bad qualities of one who, while working for the ultimate good of his country, employed methods which filled the hearts of his subjects with fear. His aim would have been considered admirable today. It was to standardize and mechanize the state until it resembled a perfectly functioning machine. As the army was the tool by which he enforced his will on others, it enjoyed pre-ferential treatment. His soldiers and the peasants who tilled the soil were the favoured citizens of the new state.

The First Supreme Divine Ruler was himself of doubtful birth, for he was reported to be the off-spring of a clever merchant and not the son of the late king of Ch'in. Therefore, with the thoroughness of one who is not sure of his own heritage, he set forth to destroy the old nobility and all those of the old order better born than himself. The written records of the Empire, in which were compiled the history and literature of a glorious past, disproved his claim to be the first ruler of the Chinese world, so they were destined to perish, along with the aristocracy and those scholars who had the courage to protest. This event, which history considers one of the greatest acts of vandalism of all times, was called 'The Burning of the Books.' The sacred books of Confucius, as well as the historical records of the past, were consumed in a holocaust of flames. In this way, with one blow, Shih Huang Ti deprived his country of the two brightest jewels in her crown: her scholars and the records of a great civilization.

A despotic administrator, whether he is an emperor or only the head of a small state, must, of necessity, use every means at his disposal to make his own position secure. As the terror which his mailed fist invoked in the hearts of his subjects seemed an insufficient protection to the First Ruler, he created imaginary terrors to further his own ends and worked upon the superstitions of his subjects. With masterly stagecraft he built for himself a palace in imitation of the World of the Immortals, where he lived an invisible existence removed from the eyes of his people. His few public appearances were arranged so that they savoured of the supernatural in an age

when quick transportation from one place to another
was unknown.

In life he was a strange, mysterious man, and his
death after eleven short years of almost superhuman
activity was as curious as his life had been. His last
resting-place was a magnificent tomb dug out of the
side of a mountain. When it was finished after his
death, and his body laid within, the entrance was
walled in with earth, and grass and shrubs were
planted so that no one should ever know where the
tomb of the Emperor was situated. Inside the tomb
huge candles made of walrus fat, the so-called everlasting lamps of antiquity, illumined a map of the
empire spread out on the ground. Winding rivers of
quicksilver flowed in and out, and mountains and
cities were pictured in relief. Stars twinkled in the
roof and were reflected in the treasures of gold and
silver piled about the body as it lay in state. To insure
that the secret of the tomb would be well kept, those
men who had worked on its construction were
trapped in the passage between the burial chamber
and the outer gate. They died with their master and
carried their knowledge with them to the grave.
Some authorities say that sundry wives and concubines were buried alive in the tomb with the Emperor
in order to accompany him on his journey to the
spirit world, but such a statement is open to question.

Huang Ti had made all the necessary preparations
for his own life after death, but he had neglected to
provide a successor capable of carrying on his work

on earth. In the state which he had created, where all the power was in the hands of one man, there was no place for other great men, no soil prepared, as it were, for brains and initiative to grow. So when he died the greatness of his house passed with him, and a few' years after his death the House of Han ruled in its stead. His mechanized, well-regulated world was not destined to survive, because it was based on fear, and when the fear was removed it crumbled and went to pieces. A period of unrest ensued, and as Confucius says in the Odes: 'When a country is about to collapse there are many conflicting administrative changes.'

These details of the life and death of Shih Huang Ti are only relevant to our story because they describe the conditions which existed during the youth of Liu Pang, the founder of the Han dynasty, and his wife, the notorious Empress Lu. At first they had suffered from the tyranny of Shih Huang Ti, but later they profited by the unrest and disintegration which surrounded them after his death. The superior men of the country had been killed, learning had been discouraged, and after eleven years of having their actions regulated by law the people had forgotten how to think for themselves. It was the moment for the rogue and the adventurer to profit, and the men who strove for power after the death of the Emperor were both.

The country was weary—weary of strife and regulations. Vast multitudes had fled to distant places, including Korea, to avoid the terror which emanated from the palace of the Emperor. Confidence had been destroyed; uncertainty veiled the future; and discontent, that forerunner of future upheavals, filled the hearts of the people. Thanks to the propaganda of Shih Huang Ti, the air was believed to be filled with demons and fairies. Magicians were called in to calm the fears of an ignorant multitude and they reaped a golden harvest from those who, with their help, sought to propitiate the powers of darkness. In an atmosphere of superstition, uncertainty, and unrest the childhood of the future Empress was spent.

The father of the Empress Lu had been a man of position and means, but it was an age when position counted for little and wealth might be here today and gone tomorrow. One man was as good as another for all intents and purposes, so this father of a marriageable daughter conceived a novel plan for selecting a son-in-law. With keen eyes and no mean knowledge of psychology, he looked into the faces of the men he saw about him—and then he chose the one he liked best for his daughter.

Liu Pang, the successful candidate, was a man of the people, and, unlike his father-in-law, he had inherited neither wealth nor position. He was a peasant, and was first heard of as the leader of a small band of men sent out to work on one of the many building projects of Shih Huang Ti, perhaps on the Great Wall itself. As many of his workmen died of hardship and overwork, those who remained alive decided to revolt, and choosing Liu Pang to be their leader, they fled to the mountains. There they remained until the death of the Emperor enabled them to return home with safety.

The hereditary nobility had disappeared, so when Liu Pang returned from the hills to P'ei, the town in which he had formerly lived, the people welcomed him as a hero. They put their own magistrate to death and Liu Pang was chosen to be the local ruler and given the title of Duke of P'ei. Eventually the new duke was put in command of the southern army of the Empire. He gathered together under his standard men like himself; men who knew what it was to be hungry and live dangerously, and who had nothing to lose and much to gain by attaching themselves to his cause.

It would seem probable in the light of subsequent events that the girl who became the wife of Liu Pang neither liked nor admired her husband. His fine beard, and his prominent nose and 'dragon's fore-head,' referred to with admiration by the historian Ssu-ma Ch'ien, can have been little compensation to her for having been married to a peasant. She was more intelligent than he, and more ruthless. Liu Pang was an easy-going, kind-hearted man while his wife was his opposite in every respect. She undoubtedly despised him because she thought him a weakling. Like many other easy-going men, he simplified life for himself by spending much time away from home. He left the care of their children to his wife while he led his armies about the country, not only during the time when he was an unknown soldier of fortune, but later, after he had been proclaimed Emperor.

It is difficult for the impartial historian to discover why Liu Pang was successful in winning the throne. According to the written records of the time he was an indifferent general. Certainly he was many times besieged and often defeated. When besieged he always managed to escape by reason of the cleverness and devotion of his friends, who used their wits to further his cause. Whenever he was defeated he would spend the ensuing period of calm in reorganizing his armies, so that he could fall upon his enemies when they least expected him to renew the attack.

His principal rival for the throne was the leader of the northern army, the general Hsiang-chi. The two men had at one time been friends, and over the camp fires of long ago they had even sworn brotherhood. This fact must be taken into consideration, for when they began to fight each other their methods of warfare resembled not so much the mortal combat of two desperate men, as a series of duels, fought between two antagonists who rather enjoy the sport and who are in no hurry to strike in a vital spot.

On one occasion Hsiang-chi had the good fortune to capture both the wife and the father of his rival, while Liu Pang himself managed to escape with his children. We do not know what happened to the future Empress during the period of her captivity, but captivity must have been grim enough at best during the third century B.C., and it is possible that the hardships she then endured unsettled her reason and were the cause of her hallucinations and insane fits of rage in later years. It could not have added to her affection for her husband to learn that he was in no hurry to have her back. Her captor, Hsiang-chi, was probably aware that no love was lost between Liu Pang and his strong-minded wife, therefore connubial bliss was not even considered to be a possible basis for military negotiations. Filial piety was substituted in its place, and Liu Pang was advised that unless his army surrendered immediately his old father would be boiled alive. Liu Pang, who was above all else a realist and anything but sentimental, hastened to dispatch the following reply:

'When in the service of the late King, you and I became sworn brothers. My father is therefore your father. However, if you do decide to boil him, let me have a basin of the broth.'

In the circumstances Hsiang-chi did not think it worth while to kill the old man, but for a long period of time kept him and the future Empress in captivity.

Eventually the war came to an end, and a truce was arranged. The father and wife were returned to Liu Pang, and when all was thought to be quiet and peace believed to be assured, he fell upon his rival and inflicted a crushing defeat. Hsiang-chi, like others who trusted to the word of Liu Pang, was caught unprepared, and when his army was destroyed he committed suicide. This left the way open for Liu Pang to proclaim himself Emperor, which he subsequently did under the name of Kao Ti. The name of Han which he gave to his dynasty was that of the river which flowed near the town where he was born.

After reading the account of this struggle between the two men, one noted for his craftiness and the other for his cruelty, one might ask, as Liu Pang afterwards asked his princes and officers: 'Why have I obtained the Empire? Why?' It would seem as if there must have been a master mind behind the web of craft and inefficiency and, indeed, his ultimate victory may have been due to the counsels of the Empress Lu. It is not difficult to imagine her thirsting to avenge the insult of her captivity and urging her husband to attack once more at any price. Honour was the last thing that bothered Liu Pang, and it is possible that he agreed to her insistent demands, as he agreed to others later in his career. What was the breaking of a truce after all compared to peace in the home, and Lu was not the woman to take an insult quietly.

Several of his lieutenants contributed not a little to his good fortune. On one occasion, when Liu Pang was undergoing a siege, one of his men disguised himself as his general and went over to the enemy to give himself up. In the confusion which followed Liu Pang managed to escape, but the unfortunate impersonator was burned alive when the ruse was discovered.

At another time, when a Hun chieftain had surrounded the army of Liu Pang, the besieged men organized a puppet show for the benefit of the enemy. A lady puppet of rare charm was successful in captivating the heart of the susceptible Hun and instilled into his breast the firm conviction that Chinese women were the most beautiful and the most desirable on earth. So pleased was he with the show that he allowed Liu Pang to escape, but later, when Liu Pang was in a position to grant the request, he sent him a demand for a Chinese princess to be his wife. The organizer of the puppet show was created a marquis as a reward for his cleverness and he became one of the band of nobles that surrounded the new Emperor when he came to the throne.

All those who had helped Liu Pang were rewarded. The old feudal titles were re-created for their benefit, and consequently a great number of former soldiers, whom a Jesuit historian describes as 'Kinglets,' strutted about the country proud of their own importance. Their wily lord, however, had no intention of allowing them to remain permanently in possession of the lands and titles he had given them. In the course of time the 'Kinglets' were quietly removed one by one to make way for princes of the House of Han. Perhaps Liu Pang, in spite of the burning of the books, knew the old Chinese proverb: 'You cannot piece out a sable robe with rats' tails.'

The task which confronted Liu Pang, or the Emperor Kao Ti, as he was now called, was no easy one. The land over which he had been called upon to rule was in a deplorable condition. Ssu-ma Ch'ien, the greatest of Chinese historians, has described the state of the country in the following words:

'When the House of Han arose, the evils of their predecessors had not passed away. Husbands still went off to the wars. The old and the young were employed in transporting food. Production was almost at a standstill, and money had become scarce. Even the Son of Heaven had not carriage-horses of the same colour; the highest civil and military authorities rode in bullock-carts, and the people at large knew not where to lay their heads.'

The Emperor set to work to restore order, but his work was hampered by the fact that he was never very sure of his own position. When he was told by his counsellors that the old capital of Loyang was not suitable for defence, he built a new one at Ch'ang-an, on the River Wei. One hundred and forty thousand people, both men and women, were conscripted to build the walls of the new city, while additional thousands constructed the Emperor's palace, which he called the Palace of Perpetual Joy.

Needless to say, all the old rules governing court etiquette had been swept away and forgotten during the long years of upheaval. The new nobles and generals, by reason of their low birth and bad manners, caused confusion in the palace. Court banquets too often resulted in drunken battles, when the walls and pillars of the palace were mistaken for imaginary enemies by over-valiant warriors. The Emperor had a suspicion that the unseemly brawls which took place detracted from the dignity of his position, and he was greatly annoyed. Although he had no faith in books nor culture he realized that something must be done, so he turned to the nearest Confucian scholar, Shu-Sen T'ung, and ordered him to find a way of maintaining order.

Shu-Sen T'ung was a man of resource; he immediately sent to the native state of Confucius for thirty scholars, with whose help he worked out a new system of ceremonial procedure. He organized a mock court which occupied itself with all the details of palace etiquette, and at the end of a month of intensive work the Emperor was invited to see the result. 'I can do it,' said Kao Ti, and he ordered all his nobles to learn the ritual. On completion of the Palace of Perpetual Joy, court ceremonies were instituted and order prevailed. The imperial censor supervised all banquets and wine was passed only nine times. Brawls and unbecoming conduct ceased and the Emperor said: 'Now I begin to understand the honour and pleasure of being an Emperor.'

Besides building and fighting, the jovial Emperor had other interests. He loved both wine and women.

The Empress Lu was getting on in years, and like other Emperors he had many concubines to bear him sons. His favourite was the concubine Ch'i, the mother of a young boy called Jou-i, whom the Emperor loved best of all his children. The Empress Lu was desperately jealous of the Lady Ch'i because she feared that Jou-i would be proclaimed Heir Apparent in place of her own son. Her fears were not without ground because the Emperor actually had proposed to change the succession, and had there not been opposition from his ministers the son of Lu would never have been allowed to come to the throne. Lu was deeply grateful to the men who had defended her son's right. They had insisted that the son of an Empress should always take precedence over the son of a concubine.

Kao Ti was a shrewd man, and it is possible that he saw the weakness of his eldest son and feared to leave the Empire to one who would inevitably be dominated by others. He knew only too well the character of his wife, the boy's mother, and he was unwilling that the Empire should slip into her cruel hands. Unfortunately, the opposition of his counsellors induced the Emperor to abandon his project for the time being. He was still a comparatively young man and doubtless thought he had many more years before him.

As long as her husband lived the Empress Lu remained in the background, and we only hear of her from time to time when some question arose regarding the future of her children. When danger threatened them she came into the open and fought like a tiger. At one time her husband wished to send her eldest daughter as bride to the chief of the Hsiung-nu tribes. Kao Ti had many excellent reasons for desiring to propitiate the Hsiung-nu. In a famous letter, Li Lang, an exile who had been made a prisoner by the Hsiung-nu after the defeat of his army, described the Emperor's own defeat at their hands.

> 'The Emperor Kao with three hundred thousand men at his back was shut up in Ping-cheng. Generals he had, like clouds, counsellors, like drops of rain. Yet he remained seven days without food and then only escaped with his life.'

This was a state of affairs which the Emperor thought should never be allowed to happen again, and with considerable foresight he conceived a vision of the future, when the Hsiung-nu tribes would be ruled over by his own descendants, the children of his daughter and the Hun chieftain. To tame and civilize the barbarians of the future by other means than warfare was a subtle plan, but it was circumvented by the Empress, who refused to allow her daughter to depart. A lady from the palace was sent to impersonate the princess, and she became the wife of the chieftain. We do not know the ultimate fate of this lady, but presumably, after a few winters in the inhospitable, bleak land of the Hsiung-nu, she, like many other Chinese women of noble birth since the time of the Emperor Kao, found a grave in the barbarians' country.

The Emperor lived only a few years after his accession to the throne. On one of his many expeditions he was hit by an arrow. The wound was not a serious one, but the journey home aggravated the trouble, and the Empress Lu hastened to send for the best doctors in the country. Kao Ti, who professed to distrust science as completely as he did literature, mocked at the learned doctors, saying:

'If I, with only a linen garment and my own sword to help me, have conquered the Empire, it must have been the will of Heaven. You can do nothing. Go away and leave me in peace.'

He died in his Palace of Perpetual Joy at the age of fifty-two, in 196 B.C., and the Empire was left in the feeble hands of his eldest son.

The question of who was going to be the master was settled quickly. The young prince was only fourteen years of age when he came to the throne, and he never had a chance against his powerful mother. He was kind-hearted and easy-going like his father before him, but with none of the personality of the latter. Women, eunuchs, and the enervating influences of palace life had done their deadly work while he was still young, and the Emperor, his father, had been away at the wars too often to counteract undesirable influences in his son's life. The Empress Lu had had to wait a long time to gratify her love of power, but with her tolerant husband out of the way she was free to throw off the mask and show her true nature. The Lady Ch'i, the concubine of the late Emperor, as well as Jou-i, her son, had long been objects of her hatred and suspicion; now she was free to have her revenge.

Jou-i had been the playmate of the young Emperor Hui since his earliest childhood, so when the Empress sent for the boy to return to the palace, the Emperor hastened out to meet his brother, and the two boys resumed their former life together. This was not at all what the Empress had desired, but she was forced to wait for her opportunity as she wished to get Jou-i out of the way as quietly as possible. There were always watchful nobles to protect the person of an imperial prince, and the Empress did not wish for any interference with her plans.

One morning the Emperor rose at an early hour to go hunting, leaving Jou-i behind him asleep. This was the moment for which the Empress Lu had been waiting. Stealthily entering the boy's apartment she woke him up and forced him to drink a glass of poisoned wine. Then, when she saw him writhing in agony at her feet, she went off to the even more congenial task of dispatching her former rival, the boy's mother. Poison was too merciful in the eyes of the Empress Lu for the Lady Ch'i, so palace eunuchs were ordered to seize the lady, her hands and feet were cut off, her eyes put out and other horrible mutilations inflicted, and in the end the body, still quivering with life, was cast upon a dung-heap to await the coming of the young Emperor.

Perhaps the Empress Lu thought to harden her son and accustom him to terrible sights when she led him to the dung-heap after he returned from hunting, but if so she was disappointed. The boy, confronted by the remains of his father's favourite wife and the body of his dead playmate, was taken ill and for over a year his health was affected. He realized for the first time that it would be hopeless for him to attempt to be Emperor in anything but name, and the terror and horror which his mother inspired in him are reflected in his words:

'This is not the work of a human being. Henceforth I will have nothing to do with affairs of state.'

He kept his word, and on his recovery gave himself up to drunkenness and debauchery, leaving everything to his mother, whom he now regarded as the emissary of the evil forces of darkness.

This double murder was the beginning of a reign of terror for all those connected with the House of Han. Such a policy on the part of the Empress can only be explained by the fact that Lu was at last able to show openly the hatred which she had always felt for her peasant husband. The destruction of his family became an obsession with her, but she was mentally too irrational to pursue a definite plan to its logical conclusion. After the death of Jou-i, another son of the late Emperor was called to the palace, imprisoned and starved to death in punishment for some imaginary offence, while a third and a fourth son were allowed to remain alive. One became a model of filial piety by refusing to change his clothes for three years after the death of his mother, a concubine of the late Emperor, while the other was called to the throne after the death of Lu.

Virtue as a means of prolonging life became popular during this despotic reign, as did a life of extreme asceticism. One grand-counsellor shut himself up in his house with the avowed intention of devoting the remainder of days to the austere observances prescribed by the Taoist religion. Others followed his example and the people realized that these men were attempting to save their own lives by relinquishing their ambitions and removing themselves from the danger zone. Even a sojourn among the nomad tribes seemed preferable to life at court, where a command was often followed by a death-warrant, and where the heads of those who displeased the Empress were exceedingly unsafe on the shoulders of their owners. Many of her murders were the result of a sudden outburst of rage, but behind the rage was usually the cunning policy of destroying the imperial dynasty and establishing her own family on the throne. The letter to which reference has already been made by Li Lang, the exiled general, although written at a later period, describes conditions as they were during the reign of the Empress Lu.

'Oh, my friend, thou sayest that the House of Han never fails to reward a deserving servant. But thou art thyself a servant of the House, and it would ill beseem thee to say other words than these. Yet Hsiao and Fan were bound in chains; Han and P'eng were sliced to death; Ch'ao Ts'o was beheaded, Chou Po was disgraced, and Tou Ying paid the penalty with his life. Others, great in their generation, have also succumbed to the intrigues of base men, and have been overwhelmed beneath a weight of shame from which they were unable to emerge.'

Occasionally the Empress Lu would allow herself to be guided by her ministers, because she was really more interested in palace intrigues than in what went on in the state. At one time the old enemy, the chief of the Hsiung-nu tribes, feeling himself strong enough to pull the lion's tail, sent an insulting letter to the Empress demanding her hand in marriage. Lu was so angry that she nearly put the envoy to death. She wished to dispatch immediately a large army with which to punish the presumptuous Hun. One of her ministers supported this policy, but a second was against it. He reminded the Empress that her husband had fought the Hsiung-nu with no success, and that the people were still singing a popular song in the streets about his defeat.

'These barbarians are beasts,' said the counsellor. 'Why be angry at their insults or rejoice in their good will?'

The Empress listened to his wise words and sent the chief a conciliatory letter protesting that the state of her teeth and hair did not allow her to compete for his affections. The letter was carried by an ambassador from the court, who took with him a present of fine horses, perhaps the same squat, bull-necked, thin-legged horses tossing their heads and foaming with impatience to be off, which Han artists loved to carve in relief on slabs of stone. In any case, the chief was flattered and he begged the Empress to overlook his bad manners, which, he said, were due to his lack of knowledge of the superior etiquette of the Chinese court.

When the Emperor was seventeen his mother, the Empress Lu, arranged a marriage for him with his niece, the daughter of his eldest sister. The event was celebrated with great rejoicings and several unpopular laws were rescinded, among which was the old law of Shih Huang Ti relating to the burning of the sacred books of Confucius. The Emperor Kao had adopted the Confucian ceremonial for his court, but he had allowed the old law to stand.

'What need have I of your book of history or your book of changes, or any of your other books?' he had exclaimed.

It was left to his descendants to gather together what was left of the ancient learning, and to have it arranged so that the wisdom of their forefathers would be available for future generations.

The year 188 B.C. began with an eclipse of the sun; an event which in ancient China was considered to be an omen of coming disaster, and when a second eclipse took place in the fifth month, everyone expected something dreadful to happen. No one was surprised when the Emperor died suddenly without leaving a son to inherit the throne. This did not disconcert the Empress Lu, who commanded her granddaughter, the young Empress, to produce an heir. A child was brought to the palace from outside and passed off as legitimate, while, as a precaution, the boy's mother was put to death. Lu had now a puppet Emperor to place on the throne, but he did not live long. In the course of time he learnt the secret of his birth and was heard to say that one day he would avenge his real mother. The remark was his death-warrant, and he was speedily removed. He was the first of five puppet Emperors, whose very names are forgotten, to be placed on the throne by the Empress Lu. The history of the Han dynasty speaks of her as the sole ruler of the state for a period of eight years; a unique honour which was never repeated during the following two thousand years of Chinese history.

After the death of her son, the Empress Lu appeared to be inconsolable and the lives of her ministers became more and more precarious. A counsellor thought to prevent trouble by removing himself and his colleagues from the chief point of danger, and he suggested that the control of the palace be turned over to the family of the Empress. The imperial grief was speedily assuaged, but from that time until her death her own family ruled the state. All her kinsmen were given positions of power, while the remaining princes of the House of Han went into retirement, and those who escaped with their lives waited in obscurity for a propitious moment to return. Probably much bloodshed was avoided by this simple expedient, but the family of the Empress paid the penalty for her crimes after her death.

In the later history of China two other Dowager Empresses imitated Lu and attempted to destroy the ruling house so that they might substitute their own. The Empress Wu of the T'ang dynasty very nearly succeeded, while in our own time Tz'u Hsi, the great Empress of the Manchu dynasty, was possessed of the same idea. Both ladies were students of history and knew all about the Empress Lu; indeed, Wu Hou was in the habit of justifying herself by pointing out the superiority of her own policy to that of her notorious predecessor. The T'ang dynasty was no doubt saved because Wu Hou feared that the fate which evertook the kinsmen of Lu might destroy her own family after her death. There are many points of similarity between the reigns of the three Empresses, and even in character they resembled each other to a certain extent. All three were domineering, cruel women, who lived only for power and who allowed nothing to stand in their way.

We can observe life as it was lived during the reigns of the Han Emperors when we visit those relics of the dynasty which have survived and which are today preserved in museums. A few drawings, some primitive sculpture, and many fine stone carvings in relief illustrate the pageantry and luxury of the age. But the Empress Lu lived during a period of transition, and life at her court could be both rough and dangerous. It was not so many years before that the Emperor Kao had objected because his drunken nobles mutilated the walls of the palace with their swords.

Liou-tchang, a young marquis of the House of Han, had taken the precaution of marrying a relative of the Empress Lu, and for that reason he had been able to maintain his position at court, where he even became a favourite of the despotic lady. She called him her cup-bearer, and allowed him certain liberties which were not accorded to the other exiled or imprisoned members of her late husband's family. One evening at a banquet the marquis suggested that it might amuse the assembled company if for once the court etiquette, installed by the Confucian scholars, was relaxed and the laws of the camp, which had previously been those of the palace, were allowed to take its place. The Empress agreed, as the camp, in her case, was not far removed from the palace, and perhaps she sometimes longed for the wild, free life of her youth.

After the winecup, filled with spiced hot wine, had been passed many times, Liou-tchang commenced to sing a song popular with the labourers in the field, 'Good crops follow good seed, but bad seed produces only tares.' The Empress Lu realized that this was an illusion to her own misdeeds, but for once she said nothing. Soon the wine proved too strong for one of the Empress's kinsmen and he left the hall. Liou-tchang ran after him, cut off his head, and carried it back to the banqueting hall for all to see. The members of the Lu clan, stupefied with terror, remained in their seats. As long as the Empress was silent no one else dared protest. But from that day onward the young marquis was feared by the family of the Empress, and with reason, as he was instrumental in eventually destroying the entire clan.

During the last years of the reign of this fierce old woman the people walked in terror of their lives, and even Heaven itself was said to be displeased. Signs were not lacking to show that the day of retribution was at hand. Trees budded in the autumn, an ancient omen indicative of coming disaster which lost none of its potency during succeeding ages, for we read that the Empress Tz'u Hsi of the Manchu dynasty was worried when she observed the same phenomena in the gardens of her own palace at the beginning of the twentieth century.

When an eclipse of the sun took place the Empress Lu feared that the wrath of Heaven was indeed directed against herself, and in an endeavour to avert misfortune, she went to the river for the purpose of ritual bathing. On the way back she had the hallucination of being attacked by a supernatural animal. Soon after she felt pain where she thought the animal had bitten her, and, thoroughly frightened, she consulted the court magicians. When she was told that the spirit of Jou-i, the murdered son of her rival, inhabited the body of the strange apparition, she knew that her end was near and prepared for death. Just before she died she instructed her kinsmen to guard the palace against a possible uprising on the part of the ministers, and to strive to establish a regency.

It was vain advice. The army, backed by the country, rose against her clan, and every man, woman and child bearing the name of Lu was exterminated. A surviving son of the Emperor Kao by a concubine was called to the throne and the House of Han returned to power. Great rulers and many scholars rank high among the prosperous descendants of Liu Pang, the crafty, good-natured peasant, but of the family of the Empress Lu not one lived to perpetuate her name.

With all her faults the rule of this Empress was beneficial for the country. The times were so bad that the people were shaken out of their lethargy and determined to remedy conditions. The new Emperor was chosen because he was already a mature man, who had shown himself endowed with wisdom and judgment. The nation was no longer willing to permit a puppet Emperor to sit upon the throne, with, perhaps, another Dowager Empress pulling the wires behind the scenes. Like King Wen, referred to in the Odes of Confucius, the new Emperor 'took virtue as his guide, and thus gradually pacified the four quarters of the world.'

Pan Chao

IV

A FEMINIST OF LONG AGO:
PAN CHAO

[48–117 A.D.]

'Honour and dishonour, poverty and wealth,
These may not be sought.
With body erect, let us walk the Way!
And bide the proper time.
Our turn of life may be long, (or) short,
The stupid and the wise are alike in this.
Let us be quietly reverential; resigned to our Destiny,
Regardless whether a good or an evil one,
Let us respect, be careful, and not be indolent;
Let us think of being humble and temperate,
Let us be pure and calm, and want little,
Like the Master Kung Ch'o.'

FROM THE POEM OF PAN CHAO CALLED
'TRAVELLING EASTWARD,' TRANSLATED
BY NANCY LEE SWANN

Characters in the Story

PAN CHAO	*Known as the Lady Ts'ao. The foremost woman scholar of China*
PAN KU	*Her brother. An historian*
PAN CH'AO	*Another brother. A general*
PAN CHIEH-YU	*Her great-aunt. Concubine of the Emperor Ch'eng of the Han Dynasty*
MA RUNG	*Pupil of Pan Chao*
THE EMPEROR HO	*Patron of Pan Chao*
THE EMPRESS TENG	*His wife. Pupil of Pan Chao*

A FEMINIST OF LONG AGO

IN the first century of our era, during the reign of the Emperor Ho of the Eastern Han dynasty, there lived in China a remarkable woman by the name of Pan Chao. She was born of a family of scholars. Her forefathers had been men of letters and her brother became the most noted historian of his day. On the distaff side of the family her great-aunt Pan Chieh-yu, the concubine of the Emperor Ch'eng of the Han dynasty, had been a woman well known for her strong character as well as for her literary gifts. Pan Chao herself appears to have inherited the talents of her famous aunt. She not only had literary ability, but she acquired immense learning during her long life and was able to assist her brother when he was appointed court historian. Later she wrote a book of instructions for women which became a classic for the training of girls. Her reasoning and her advice were so sound that her book is still read in China to this day. It is from this book and from her poems that we are able to reconstruct the story of her life.

The imperial concubine Pan Chieh-yu, the great-aunt of Pan Chao, had established the fortunes of the

Pan family on the basis of royal favour as for a long time she had been the most influential concubine at the court, and it was doubtless due to her efforts that her brothers were given positions by the Emperor. She must have felt very sure of her own power, for once she even rebuked the Emperor publicly. This, of course, was a grave mistake. The incident is depicted on the famous Ku K'ai-Chih scroll-painting on view in the British Museum.

In this picture, which is attributed to the fourth-century artist Ku K'ai-Chih, we see a determined little lady with flying draperies and flowing robes. Looking down on her from his litter, borne high on the shoulders of stalwart litter-bearers, is her husband, the Emperor. The picture bears this legend: 'The refusal of Pan Chieh-yu to ride in the litter of the Emperor.' We learn from the inscription that she had just addressed the Emperor in these words:

'In old paintings wise and great princes have always had illustrious ministers seated beside them: not favourites as in more degenerate days.'

The Ku K'ai-Chih scroll adds this illuminating commentary:

'When the concubine Pan made a certain answer she deprived herself of the pleasure of riding in the Emperor's carriage. Was it because she did not appreciate the honour? No. It was because she had foresight and wished to prevent scandal.'

Pan Chieh-yu was successful in preventing scandal, but the Emperor soon wearied of her good advice and she found herself supplanted in his affections by the famous dancer known as the Flying Swallow. The dancer wanted to change the highly moral atmosphere of the court to one which was better suited to both herself and the Emperor, but she realized that to do so she must first have the Empress and Pan Chieh-yu sent away. To their great surprise the ladies found themselves accused of witchcraft. Pan Chieh-yu was clever enough to clear herself of the charge, but the Empress was disgraced, and the concubine chose to follow her into exile. As a protest Pan Chieh-yu composed a poem which she sent to the Emperor written on a fan. In the poem she compares herself to a fan which has been discarded when the heat of the summer has passed, and which is laid aside as of no longer any use to its owner. The term 'autumn fan' has passed into the Chinese language as a descriptive phrase for a deserted wife.

It may have been that the conscience of the Emperor was troubled by the poem, or he may have realized that he had treated the lady badly. In any case he presented to the Pan family some exceedingly valuable ancient manuscripts from the imperial library which had hitherto been inaccessible to scholars. These priceless manuscripts were the foundation on which the subsequent literary fame of the Pan family rested. They were passed from the brother of the imperial concubine to the father of Pan Chao, and later to her own brother Pan Ku, and in this way became the link which bound the three generations together.

Pan Chao had two brothers who were both destined to become celebrated men, Pan Ku, the historian, and Pan Ch'ao, who later became a famous general. The brothers were older than their sister, and it is said that as a small child she was in the habit of hiding behind a curtain while they were at their lessons, and that is how she learned to read. When it was discovered that she already knew a number of characters she was given an instructress by her father and until the age of fourteen she was allowed to devote herself to her beloved books. It is easy to imagine that the brothers took great pride in the progress made by their talented sister, and in later years Pan Ku requested her assistance when he was writing the history of the Han dynasty.

Fourteen was the age for a girl to marry, and at fourteen Pan Chao left her home to 'take up the dustpan and broom' in the Ts'ao family. In her own home, where culture was all important, she had been allowed time to study. Now all was changed. From morning until night she 'laboured without confessing weariness.' Writing years later in the introduction to her book of instructions for women she says:

'During this time with trembling heart I feared constantly that I might disgrace my parents. Day and night I was distressed in heart.'

What a picture those words give of a timid young girl, flying about the house to answer the calls of an imperious mother-in-law. She considered herself as the humblest of that lady's servants, and she strove in every way to please her. At the same time she served to the best of her ability the young man, still a stranger to her, to whom she had been given as wife. She had been trained in the strict Confucian code of superiority and inferiority, and she says:

'If a wife does not serve her husband, then the natural order of things is neglected and destroyed.'

In her book she tells other women what not to do when they are married, and one is inclined to wonder if Pan Chao learned her wisdom by making mistakes. 'Don't follow the husband about the house, as that encourages familiarity and lust. Don't indulge in quarrels and accusations. Don't let contempt for the husband creep into the heart.' Possibly she had stumbled into all the pitfalls she advised others to avoid before love for her husband came to her. That it did come seems evident from her quotation of the following poem:

'*Should two hearts harmonize,*
The united strength can cut gold.
Words from hearts which agree,
Give forth fragrance like the orchid.'

101

Pan Chao had much to say in her book about the position of the young wife in relation to her brothers- and sisters-in-law. In a Chinese household, where all the clan lived under the same roof, separated from each other by a series of courtyards, there would, of necessity, be a great number of young people of both sexes. The young wife must make herself loved and respected by those of her own generation if she wished to make a satisfactory place for herself in her new home:

'To win for herself the love of her parents-in-law, she (the young wife) must secure for herself the good will of younger brothers- and sisters-in-law. . . . Then the excellence and the beauty of such a daughter-in-law becomes generally known. Moreover, any flaws and mistakes are hidden and unrevealed. Praise of her radiates, making her illustrious in district and neighbourhood; and her brightness reaches to her own father and mother.'

These quotations from her own book give us the history of the youth of Pan Chao. She succeeded in gaining the esteem of her husband's family, and during the years that she spent in their midst her reputation as a model daughter-in-law, wife and mother grew steadily. After the birth of her children she nursed and cared for them herself and later took complete charge of their education.

Little is known about her children except that one

son eventually received a government post and was made a marquis. As there is no record of his being a man of outstanding ability, the honour was probably an indirect compliment to his famous and exceedingly modest mother. She writes of him:

'Now that he is a man and able to plan his own life,
I need not again have concern for him.'

But a long poem which she wrote called 'Travelling Eastward' speaks of accompanying him from the capital to a distant provincial post. That she did not want to go, but from some reason considered it her duty to do so, is evident from the following lines:

'Already we leave the old and start for the new.
I am uneasy in mind, and sad at heart.'

Pan Chao had the misfortune to lose her husband early in life. It is not known when his death occurred, but after the period of mourning was over she was given permission by her husband's family to take up her residence at the home of her brother, Pan Ku. This was an unusual step for a widow to take and could only have been justified by the fact that Pan Ku needed an assistant to help him with his work on the Han Annals and that his sister with her decided literary gifts was competent to aid him. Undoubtedly the change was welcome to Pan Chao as the position of a widow in her husband's family was at best a difficult one, and she must have longed for useful work which could make her forget her sorrow. There was no question of remarriage for a woman like Pan Chao, who was a follower of Confucius and whose life was an example for other women who strove to follow in the footsteps of the great teacher.

Pan Ku, the brother, was at that time court historian and engaged in the task of completing the Han Annals. His appointment was all the more important because he had been chosen to resume the work of the historian Ssu-ma Ch'ien, which had been interrupted by the death of the latter during the previous century. Ssu-ma Ch'ien was the greatest of all the Chinese historians. That part of his history which has been translated into French gives a vivid picture of the life and social conditions of his country from prehistoric ages to the time of his death. His history and that of his successor Pan Ku were the work of men of immense learning who were qualified to write about almost every field of human knowledge. Mathematics, music, astronomy, law, economics, state sacrifices, geography, and land drainage were some of the many subjects upon which the historian was required to be an expert, while a knowledge of the classics and philosophy was expected as a matter of course.

To be confronted with such a formidable mass of material would have discouraged most women at the beginning, but Pan Chao was not easily dismayed and she possessed both courage and perseverance. During the years that she worked with her brother she became an invaluable assistant, so much so that he never failed to praise her to others and speak of her share in his work. Even the Emperor was from time to time shown extracts from the history written by Pan Chao. It was fortunate that she had these years of preparation under the supervision of her brother, for after his death she was obliged to finish the history alone. The books on astronomy, and the 'eight tables,' a record of famous people associated with the House of Han, were the parts completed by Pan Chao, while it is possible that she was obliged to edit the entire work.

After the death of Pan Ku, which occurred in A.D. 92, it was several years before his sister was called upon to resume his work. During this period of enforced idleness she accompanied her son on the journey to which we have already referred and wrote her famous poem called 'Travelling Eastward.' But eventually the Emperor summoned her to court and commanded her to finish the history. A small gallery at one end of the imperial library was turned over to her for her use, and there she gathered together all her brother's scattered manuscripts and settled down to work with ten scholars as her advisers and assistants. What she wrote was at times so complicated that only those men whom she had personally instructed could understand it.

When the history was finished it was first shown to the Emperor for his approval and then published under the name of Pan Ku. Although given to the world as the work of her brother, his sister had become famous throughout the Empire for the part she had played in completing and editing the work. The history written by the Pan family reconstructed all that had happened of interest during the Han dynasty, that is to say, over a space of two hundred and thirty years, from the time of the Emperor Kao, founder of the dynasty, until the reign of the Emperor Ho, the patron of Pan Chao. It had been a period of extraordinary prosperity, and the record was one that the rulers of the Han dynasty could be proud to hand down to posterity. The work was considered so important by scholars that among the learned men of Pan Chao's generation 'there was none but read it.' This history has served as a model for subsequent dynastic chronicles, which, taken as a whole, carry the history of China down to the present day;—the longest narrative of events that has ever been compiled and preserved by any nation.

When Pan Chao took up her residence at court, she was exceedingly fortunate to find that the Empress shared her scholarly tastes. This young woman had recently been a concubine, and when she had entered the place, she alone among all the gorgeously-clad ladies of the court dressed simply and wore no jewels. It was her qualities of mind and heart that won for her the affection of the Emperor and it was not long before she was given the rank of Empress. In her childhood the Empress Teng had been given an opportunity to study and she wished to continue under the direction of Pan Chao. So the Emperor commanded the historian to teach his young and beautiful wife poetry, elocution, and history. Many of the court ladies followed the example of the Empress and became the pupils of Pan Chao, and something like a palace revolution took place in the habits of the court. It may have been that Pan Chao wrote her book of instructions for women for the benefit of her young and frivolous pupils as well as for the girls of her own family.

One of the sections of the Ku K'ai-Chih scroll is devoted to the portrait of a lady who is designated as the instructress of the ladies in the palace. There is no evidence that this is a picture of Pan Chao, but it is of interest as it proves that an instructress in the palace was required to wear the long gown of the court lady and that she dressed her hair with large jewelled ornaments. In spite of all her learning Pan Chao must have been essentially a woman to have been able to wear this impracticable costume with dignity and grace after a life spent in seclusion and useful work. How she ever found time for an elaborate toilet apart from all the other duties which devolved on her at court is explained in the introduction to her book in the following words:

'Let a woman retire late to bed, but rise early to duties; let her not dread tasks by day or night.'

When Pan Chao became the instructress of the

Empress, the Emperor Ho conferred on her a title
which had never before been given to any woman.
She was called the Lady Ts'ao. But Pan Chao had
never cared for honours or titles. She was content to
remain the most modest of women and to prove herself worthy of the high reputation which she enjoyed.
In the introduction to her book she speaks of herself
as being 'careless and by nature stupid,' and in her
memorials to the throne she calls herself, 'Your hand-
maiden, worm that she is.' It was this modesty which
made her prefer to devote the greater part of her life
to assisting her brother, although she herself possessed
the qualities which would have made her an author
of the first rank. The most important work to appear
under her own name was her book of instructions for
women, which was written, not to enhance her own
reputation, but solely for the guidance and help of
others.

When the book of instructions was finished, Pan
Chao, ever doubtful of her own ability, wished to
have the opinion of some experienced person, so she
showed it to her pupil, Ma Rung, a man who had
already achieved fame as a scholar. Ma Rung was so
impressed with the book that he made a copy of it
with his own hand and ordered his wife to learn it
by heart. Other scholars followed his example and
everyone hoped that a reformation in the customs of
the home would result. It is possible that this book
was one of the first to have been written on paper, as
paper was a new invention and had only been brought

to the attention of the court in A.D. 105. When the Empress Teng entered the palace and the Emperor Ho wished to shower gifts upon her, it is recorded that she chose to keep only writing brushes and paper, and returned the jewels and fine silks. The choice is not so surprising when it is realized what a novelty paper must have been.

Towards the end of the long life of Pan Chao the Emperor died, and the Empress Teng, her pupil, became the regent for her young son. This lady, who was something of a mystic and seems to have had unusual penetration when it came to reading the hearts of men, instituted many reforms. She was able to separate the honest from the dishonest officials after a glance at their faces. During her reign so many economies were instituted that she was able to return half of the tribute sent yearly by the different provinces of the Empire. It was her custom to consult Pan Chao upon affairs of state, and in the Empress's biography it is written that 'at one word from mother Pan the whole family resigned.' This remark refers to an incident when the Empress's elder brother wished to retire from office and was only given official permission to do so after Pan Chao had presented a memorial to the throne, giving good and sufficient reasons why the request should be granted. It is interesting to note that Pan Chao, although primarily a woman of letters, possessed considerable political ability. As was the case with so many Chinese men, her knowledge of the classics and her training as a scholar proved to be the best preparation for a career in the world of politics.

We have one more glimpse of the political activities of Pan Chao. This relates to another memorial addressed to the throne requesting the recall of her second brother who, for many years, had been serving his country on the borders of the Empire. In his youth this brother had been very poor and had been forced to take a position as a copyist in a government office. His biographer says:

'One day after a long period of hard labour, he stopped his task, threw down his brush, sighed and said: "How can one live long between the brush and the ink slab?" When those about him laughed Pan Ch'ao said: "You little people, how can you know the purpose of a strong man?" '

The 'strong man' was later sent on a mission to Eastern Turkestan, where he spent the greater part of his life. Like his brother and sister, he possessed exceptional ability, and he rose in rank until he became a famous general. Later he was made governor-general of Eastern Turkestan and was ennobled with the rank of marquis. The general carried the cultural ideals of the Han Empire to distant parts of the world, and his fame rested quite as much on his statesmanship as on his ability as a soldier. At the age of seventy, old, tired and ill, he wished to retire, but it was a long time before those in authority could decide to dispense with his services. In the memorial addressed to the throne his sister writes:

'He is hard pressed by old age, and like a horse or dog (that has long served its master) he has lost his teeth.'

General Pan Ch'ao was allowed to return home, but it was already too late, for he died very soon after.

At the age of seventy Pan Chao herself died, and was mourned by all who knew her. The Empress, who had been deeply attached to her instructress, wore half-mourning, and the young Emperor sent a representative to perform funeral ceremonies before her bier. He paid the expenses of her burial, a heavy item in Chinese economic life, and showed his appreciation of her genius and integrity in other ways as well. The *literati* of her day immortalized her in prose and verse, nothing of which, unfortunately, has come down to us, and the only personal tribute which remains is the long epitaph written by her daughter-in-law, translated by the Jesuits and recorded in their history. The last words of the epitaph are:

'She (Pan Chao) lived to an extreme old age, engaged in work and happy in her virtue. Always at peace with herself as well as with others.'

Only a woman at peace with herself could have accomplished the work undertaken by Pan Chao. She combined with the duties of a wife and mother the heavy labours of an historian and writer, not to mention the duties of her position as instructress to the Empress and the young ladies of the court. This inner peace came to her as she walked the path prescribed by the great teacher Confucius. In her youth she had had opportunities to study other schools of philosophy, and although she had thoroughly acquainted herself with their esoteric meaning it was the wisdom of the Master which ruled her life. Her writings are permeated with his symbolism. In one of the Odes Confucius says:

'We may gaze up to the mountain brow; we may travel along the great road; signifying that although we cannot hope to reach the goal, still we may push on thitherward in spirit.'

Pan Chao refers to the 'great road' in her poem, 'Travelling Eastward,' when she says:

'Throughout the journey we follow the great highway.
If we seek short cuts, whom should we follow?
Pressing forward we travel on and on.'

The teachings of Confucius were so reasonable and so wise that it is not surprising to find both scholars and the common people consulting them as the ultimate source of all wisdom. Scattered through the records of Chinese history are stories not only of men but also of women who followed the 'Great Highway.' Pan Chao and the Empress Teng were two such women; women who would instinctively and without comment accept death in place of dishonour. They are far more representative of their sex and their nation than the occasional bloodthirsty Empress Dowager whose crimes were the exception and not the rule.

Pan Chao wrote three other poems. 'A Bird from the Far West,' written when her brother, the governor-general of Eastern Turkestan, presented a strange bird to his sovereign. 'The Cicada,' a poem about 'that sombre-coloured insect which, although the least and the lowliest, still derives its life from Heaven and Earth.' And the poem to 'The Needle and the Thread,' the most famous of the three:

'*Strong Spirit of Pure Steel from autumn's metal cast,*
'*(Incarnate) body (of Power), slight and subtle, straight and sharp!*
'*Things far apart all strung into one (that is your task).*'

These poems are filled with allusions to virtue and harmony, ideals which the followers of Confucius strove to emulate during the age of the Han.

In her ideas of education Pan Chao was far in advance of her time. She thought that girls between the ages of eight and fifteen should be taught the same subjects as their brothers. Not only their minds, but the care of their bodies interested her, and she tells them to wash their hair and bathe frequently, advice which should have been unnecessary in an age when government officials were given every fifth day as a holiday in order to enable them to wash their hair. The famous toilet scene from the Ku K'ai-Chih scroll bears the following inscription, which, although not written by Pan Chao, certainly expressed her sentiments:

'Men and women know how to adorn their faces, but there is none who knows how to adorn his soul.'

Like her master Confucius, Pan Chao gave practical advice which could be followed with advantage by women, irrespective of the station in life to which they belonged. If her scholarship resulted in complicated and difficult prose, it is even more to her credit that her book of instructions should have been written so clearly and so simply as to be understood by all.

The Han age was remarkable in more ways than one. The luxury of the imperial palaces, the wealth of the nation, and the fame which these years of prosperity brought to the Empire have assumed an almost legendary character. As an additional glory there were numerous poets and scholars who wrote and sang about this golden age and sculptors who left behind them works of unsurpassed beauty carved on stone. Not the least in importance among the men and women who worked together to augment the fame of the dynasty was Pan Chao, whose quiet voice can still be heard speaking to the hearts of women.

The Lady Chao on her way to the nomad chief

V

PRINCESSES IN EXILE

'Riding towards the north,
  Watched through the darkness by the desert stars,
  I think of her who, desolate, alone,
  Halted her camel here.

Like flowers below the moon
  The beauty of all other maidens seemed
  To one who looked a moment on her face.

Yet under these cold stars she came to die
  Here, where I draw my rein, remembering her.'

FROM A KOREAN POEM BY SO-KOON.
RENDERED INTO ENGLISH VERSE BY
JOAN S. GRIGSBY

Characters in the Story

THE LADY CHAO	*Concubine to the Han Emperor, Yuan*
THE PRINCESS I CHENG	*Of the Sui dynasty*
THE PRINCESS WEN-CH'ENG	*Of the T'ang dynasty*
THE LADY COCACHIN	*Of the Yuan dynasty*

V

PRINCESSES IN EXILE

Moon over the houses of Han, over the site of Ch'in.
'It flows as water—its brightness shone on Ming Fei, the
    "Bright Concubine,"
Who took the road to the Jade Pass.
She went to the edge of Heaven, but she did not return;
She gave up the moon of Han, she departed from the
    Eastern Sea.
The "Bright Concubine" married in the West, and the
    day of her returning never came.'

THE 'Bright Concubine' referred to by Li T'ai-po
in this poem was the Lady Chao of the Han dynasty,
one of the many Chinese princesses who took the
road to the frontier, poetically called the Jade Gate.
Their story is all the more pathetic because they remained silent. So strong was their loyalty to their
Emperor, so rigid their upbringing in the self-
sacrificing code of Confucius, that no thought of disobedience ever occurred to them and only here and
there a stray sentence in history or legend betrays
their sad fate. Like many European princesses they
were sent away from home for political reasons, but

their fate was harder than that of their Western sisters, because they went as brides to the chief of some nomad horde with whom their Emperor wished to make an alliance. They left luxurious and cultured surroundings to make their homes in tents under the sky, and like the Lady Chao their graves were usually in the sands of the barbarians' country.

Most of the princesses were daughters of Emperors, but the Lady Chao of the Han dynasty was an imperial concubine, although a concubine in name only, as she never saw the Emperor until the day when she set forth on her long journey. She was the daughter of educated parents, brought up in the strictest Confucian manner.

'She did not speak loudly nor did she look beyond the doors, indeed, even within the house, she only walked the path which led to her mother's room. Her ears were closed to all distracting sounds, therefore her heart and mind were pure like those of the Immortals.'

She was the joy of her father's heart and his greatest treasure, worthy to be sent as an offering to the Son of Heaven himself. That being the case, she was given to the Emperor Yuan, of the Han dynasty, who took her into his harem.

The lady was as beautiful as she was virtuous, but neither her beauty nor her virtue helped her when she reached the palace. There were so many other imperial concubines, so many other women of all ranks and grades, that the Emperor was in the habit of having their portraits painted and sent to him to choose from before the ladies themselves were summoned to his presence. If the court painter had been honest all would have been well, as no other concubine possessed the beauty of the Lady Chao, but unfortunately the loveliness of the portrait depended on the length of the model's purse and it was against the principles of the Lady Chao to give a bribe. He will paint me as I am, she must have thought, and being confident of her own charms, the artist received no extra pay. Perhaps she realized later that she had made a mistake, for the portrait submitted to the Emperor was passed over and while others were taken to his inner apartments, the Lady Chao waited in the women's courts of the palace for a call which never came.

At the end of seven years an ambassador arrived from the Hsiung-nu to demand a princess for his chief. The catalogue of portraits was consulted, and the choice fell on the Lady Chao as the least attractive of all the ladies in the harem. She was told to prepare herself for her long journey to the land of the nomads, and when the day of departure dawned she presented herself, as was the custom, before the Emperor to thank him for his kindness.

At the sight of her beauty the Emperor was amazed. Here was the loveliest lady of his court about to be turned over to the envoys of the barbarian chief. He wanted to keep her for himself now that he had seen her and he offered a camel-load of gold as a ransom, but it was refused. The envoys, too, were pleased with the beauty of the Lady Chao. They felt that their mission had been a success and they were anxious to be off with their prize.

So the Lady Chao rode away on the back of a camel and, as the poet says: 'The day of her returning never came.' It was no help to her that the guilty painter was executed and his wealth sent to her parents to console them for her loss; she was gone beyond recall. She left all those she loved to go to an alien land as the wife of an old chief with whom she had no language in common, to live among women who doubtless regarded her with suspicion and distrust. No wonder she suffered so acutely from homesickness that her name has been associated with sadness and tears ever since. While her husband lived she performed her duties as best she could, but when he died she killed herself by taking poison. Although she was buried in the desert, it is said that the mound above her grave remained for ever green.

The Hsiung-nu to whom the Lady Chao was sent were nomad tribes living on the far side of the great wall, among the deserts and steppes of the desolate country which borders China to the north and west, and which has made a barrier that for centuries prevented the Empire from making enduring contacts with other civilized countries. Up and down the steppes and the desert mounted hordes of men with their tents and beasts moved from place to place, searching for pasture or for smaller tribes to conquer. Sometimes the chief of one horde would be stronger than the others, and then his rivals would join with him to form a greater horde, and they would harass the Chinese border under one banner. The rich lands of the Chinese people were always a coveted prize in the eyes of the nomads, and it was easy for them on their swift horses to make a raid, burn and plunder, and return to their own lands before their victims could organize a defence.

The Hsiung-nu at the time of the Han, like so many other tribes called by different names at different times, lived in tents made of skins or felt which could be moved from place to place. Sometimes these tents would be fifty feet long, large enough to accommodate an entire family, but they were all built on the same pattern, with a stove near the entrance, and stones or dried dung piled round the edge to keep out the wind. The tribes possessed no written language and their communications were always by word of mouth. All grown men, strong enough to bend a bow, were soldiers, and one and all fed on the flesh of their herds and mare's milk. They used the skins of their slaughtered animals as clothing and wore overcoats of felt made out of the hair. The fighting-men received the best of everything while the others subsisted on what was left. Their chief, or Jenuye, as he called himself, which meant 'Heaven's Son Immense,' ruled the central portion of the nomad kingdom and two subordinate rulers assisted him in the east and west.

Among their many strange customs was one that greatly offended the Chinese. When the father of a family died, the son or nephew took over at least one of his wives to be his own, and in a land where men lived short and violent lives it was not uncommon for a woman to have four or five husbands, one after the other. Any Chinese princess was considered above the usual run of women, more on the level with a fine horse, and therefore exceedingly desirable. She was always the paternal widow to be passed on. This was, of course, entirely contrary to the teachings of Confucius, who said that women should never remarry, least of all one near of kin. Had the Lady Chao not committed suicide she would doubtless have been handed from chief to chief like so many others, perhaps receiving a visit twice in the year from her husband. Occasionally an unfortunate princess would object and would write to the Chinese court for instructions, but the invariable reply was to follow the customs of the country.

We learn a good deal about the Hsiung-nu from a eunuch of the Chinese court who went to the land of the barbarians in the suite of another Han princess. This man objected strongly to being banished from court and he murmured something about causing trouble for the Empire as he rode away. He kept his word, for he made friends with the Jenuye and amused himself in his exile by instructing the nomad in his dealings with the Chinese officials. He left behind a long account of their way of life:

'Their custom,' he said, 'is to eat the flesh and drink the milk of their flocks and herds, which move about after pasture according to season. Every man is a skilful bowman, and in times of peace takes life easily and happily. Though wives are taken over by sons and brethren, it is done in order to retain kith and kin all in the family: it may be incest, but it keeps up the clan stock. In China, on the other hand, though (nominally at least) sons and brothers are not incestuous, the result is estrangements, feuds, and the breaking up of the family.'

Another famous exile who lived among the nomads for many years and raised a large family by his Hsiung-nu wife was the unfortunate general Li Lang. This man was taken prisoner by the Hsiung-nu after the defeat of his army, and as was the case with many other Chinese officials who suffered the same fate, his entire family was executed by order of the Emperor. In a letter to a friend he records his grief and the sadness of his life:

'Ever since the hour of my surrender until now, destitute of all resources, I have sat alone with the bitterness of my grief. All day long I see none but barbarians around me. Skins and felt protect me from wind and rain. With mutton and whey I satisfy my hunger and slake my thirst. Companions with whom to wile time away, I have none. The whole country is stiff with black ice. I hear naught but the moaning of the bitter autumn blast, beneath which all vegetation has disappeared. I cannot sleep at night. I turn and listen to the distant sound of Tartar pipes, to the whinnying of Tartar steeds. In the morning I sit up and listen still, while tears course down my cheeks. O Tzu-ching, of what stuff am I, that I should do aught but grieve?'

The idea of sending a princess as a symbol of good will, along with rolls of silk, rice-wine, and other forms of tribute which went yearly to the Hsiung-nu in order to keep them quiet, seemed a good one to Liu Pang, the peasant founder of the Han dynasty. His reasoning was sound. 'Why not,' he said, 'have a descendant of a Han Emperor ruling over the tribes of the Hsiung-nu? In time they will become more civilized and leave the Empire alone.' Like many other good ideas this one did not materialize quite as its originator had hoped, but sometimes a remarkable leader was the result of such a mixed union. China found herself conquered on more than one occasion by a descendant of the Hsiung-nu or some other nomad tribe, who seated himself on the dragon throne and called himself a Son of Heaven.

In time the traffic in princesses assumed a form of

blackmail, and the chief of a horde wrote as follows
to the Emperor of China:

'I propose to have a frontier trade with China on
a large scale, to marry a Chinese princess, to receive annually ten thousand firkins of spirits, ten
thousand pieces of assorted silk, besides all the rest
as provided by previous treaties; if this is done we
will not raid the frontier.'

Presumably a princess was sent, for the last thing
that any Emperor wanted was to have the frontier
raided. In the third century B.C. part of the great wall
was built, and when it was completed during the
following centuries it stretched for three thousand
miles from the sea to the Gobi desert. It does not
seem, however, to have been an altogether effective
barrier against the nomads, and sometimes, when the
Empire included lands to the north of the wall, there
was no barrier at all. The system of sending princesses
and tribute was, in the long run, more satisfactory.

During the terrible centuries of upheaval and unrest which followed the fall of the Han Empire, the
Hsiung-nu were conquered by the Tartars and consequently their importance diminished. But there was
little difference between the two peoples and one
horde of nomads could be just as much a thorn in the
flesh of the Empire as another. The same methods
were used to propitiate both. When the Sui dynasty
was in power the Princess I Cheng was sent with the

accustomed tribute, but having more sense and more spirit than the Lady Chao, though perhaps less virtue, she did not waste her time in tears but made a place for herself in her new home and played the part of an efficient spy for the Chinese.

The Sui Emperor reigning at the time was the imperial madman Yang Ti. The dynasty crashed to ruin in his hands, for he was more interested in having artificial leaves attached to the trees in his gardens during the winter than in the ordinary business of running the state. When once he made an indiscreet sally into the lands of the nomads, he found himself cut off and surrounded by the Tartars, and had not the Princess I Cheng warned him in time to retreat to a neighbouring fort, he would have been cut to pieces with all his men. Shut up in the fort he could think of nothing better to do than to ask the princess to continue to help him, and again I Cheng proved equal to the occasion. She sent a message to her husband, the Tartar chief, saying that a hostile tribe was advancing against him from the north, and the chief, afraid that he might be caught between two armies, hastily retreated. The Emperor profited by the lifting of the siege to hasten home.

The Lady I Cheng had a remarkable matrimonial career, as she was married first to one chief, then to his son, and afterwards to two of her first husband's brothers. As long as the Sui dynasty remained on the throne, she used all her influence to keep the Tartars friendly with China, but after the fall of her family she became the relentless enemy of the House of T'ang. Many of her own clan took refuge with her in the days of their misfortune, including the Sui Empress, the wife of Yang Ti. In the end, when the tribe of her fourth husband was totally defeated, she was killed during the retreat.

In A.D. 641, when the Sui dynasty had ceased to exist, and the great Li Shih-min sat on the throne of China as the Emperor T'ang T'ai Tsung, second Emperor of the T'ang dynasty, a new matrimonial market was opened for imperial princesses. At that time the Tibetans sent envoys to the Emperor at Ch'ang-an to demand a wife for their king. T'ang T'ai Tsung thought their request insolent, and not being a man to be impressed by threats, he refused. A few years later, when the Tibetans had been thoroughly defeated by the T'ang armies and were in a more humble frame of mind, the Emperor was disposed to listen graciously to their request. It was agreed that he should send a member of his own family, the Princess Wen-ch'eng, as bride to Song-tsen Gam-po, their king.

Nomad blood ran in the veins of the members of the House of T'ang, as the mother of the first Emperor had been a Tartar lady, and it is possible that the Princess Wen-ch'eng inherited some of the spirit of her ancestors, for almost superhuman courage was necessary to face the future chosen for her by the Emperor. In the seventh century Tibet was just emerging from a state of barbarism. Like the Hsiung-

nu and other nomad tribes, the Tibetans had no
written language and their country had been inaccessible to the Chinese up to this time. Most of their
history was of a legendary character, and Song-tsen
Gam-po was the first king about whom any definite
information is known. The prospect of a journey to
such a land was enough to daunt the most fearless, yet
this girl, who was probably not more than fourteen
years of age, was called upon to leave her home and
go into the unknown for life-long exile. There were
other suitors from more civilized lands who asked for
her hand, but it is possible that the Emperor chose
her for this especially hard task because she was better
fitted for it than her sisters.

The journey with its detours was more than two
thousand miles long, and at the average rate of twelve
miles a day it would have taken at least seven months
to complete. When the party set out from Ch'ang-an,
Wen-ch'eng was carried in a covered chair borne by
litter-bearers, while her suite rode beside her;
camels and pack-horses carried her dowry and
presents for the king. The road she took was one that
has been used by travellers ever since. The party went
north to the province of Kansu, and then for a time
they followed the old caravan route under blazing
skies through the desert until at last they turned south
towards Amdo in Tibet. Great rivers had to be
forded which were swollen by the melting snows of
spring, the season chosen to traverse this part of the
country, for during the winter months the mountain

passes which had yet to be crossed were blocked with ice and snow. Their route took them over the Tang La Mountains, where icy winds and bitter cold greeted them sixteen thousand feet above the sea, and where Wen-ch'eng was forced to leave her covered chair and plod with the others over the passes on foot. At night her shelter was a small tent and her bed consisted of furs placed on the frozen ground.

It can have been small consolation to her that she was passing through some of the most beautiful country in the world, a country that has ever since beckoned to the explorer as the Mecca of his dreams, and which remains in parts today as remote and unknown as it was in the days of the T'ang Empire. Bears and other wild animals could only have added to her uneasiness, while the first natives she saw had their faces smeared with paint, a custom which, as she wrote back to Ch'ang-an, she considered disgusting. Month after month passed and the little party trudged on. Finally, when the blue waters of the Tengi-nor appeared on the south they knew that there was only one more range of mountains to be crossed before Lhasa would lie before them in the distance.

Most women would not have survived this terrible journey, or, if they had, they would have been so weakened by exposure as to suffer from it for the rest of their lives. But this was not the case with the Princess Wen-ch'eng. She was of different stock, and she had her faith, a firm belief in the Lord Buddha.

There was no palace to receive her when she arrived, no luxuries to compensate her for the discomforts of her long trip, but even so, this young girl did not despair. Instead of giving way to tears, she made up her mind to reform her new country, and to regenerate it as best she could.

Song-tsen Gam-po, her husband, was nineteen years of age when this Chinese princess arrived at Lhasa. He already had another wife, a Nepalese lady, and his two wives had one thing in common at least, their religion. The Nepalese princess had a nasty temper, but she agreed with Wen-ch'eng, although bitterly jealous of her, that their mutual husband as well as his country must be civilized. They persuaded him to build them a palace, and this he did on the site of the present Potala at Lhasa. It was built as a fort, but it had living accommodations and was a vast improvement on what Wen-ch'eng found on her arrival.

The next step was to convert the king to their own religion. Both ladies were ardent, one might almost say fanatical Buddhists, and at their request Song-tsen Gam-po sent one of his trusted men to India to bring back the sacred scriptures. Before they could be translated it was necessary for a written language to be created. As the Tibetans had no alphabet, letters based on the Indian alphabet as used in Kashmir were invented. The king was so pleased with all he heard from his two wives that, not to be outdone, he decided to learn reading and writing himself, and to accomplish this task he went into retirement for four years.

Wen-ch'eng proved herself to be a most industrious woman. She taught her husband's subjects to make beer out of barley and the use of butter and cheese as variations of a monotonous diet. Buddhist pilgrims followed in the trail of the sacred books coming from India and introduced pottery-making and weaving. All her life Wen-ch'eng worked unceasingly to civilize the people among whom she made her home, and it is not surprising that she became an object of respect and veneration to them. After her death she was canonized under the name of the White Tara, while the Nepalese princess was known as the Green Tara.

Song-tsen Gam-po spent most of his life fighting his enemies, but he found time between battles to make a list of the virtues which he wished his people to practise. Number thirteen is 'to be free from jealousy, and live in harmony with all,' while fourteen is short but to the point: 'Never listen to the words of women.' Most of these virtues suggest the influence of Wen-ch'eng, but number thirteen sounds like a hint for the Nepalese wife, who was noted for her jealousy and bad temper, and it is difficult to imagine that Wen-ch'eng wrote the fourteenth, because if ever a man listened to the words of a woman it was Song-tsen Gam-po himself.

Wen-ch'eng and the Nepalese princess were responsible for the introduction of Buddhism into

Tibet, and while they did not succeed in having it accepted as the permanent religion of the country during their lifetime, shrines and temples were built and several of the scriptures were translated. However, the ladies had planted the seeds which were to grow and flourish several generations later, when Tibet became the haven of refuge for the lights of Buddhism, driven into exile by a hostile Indian ruler.

But even the journey to far-away Tibet was a comparatively short one compared to the one taken by another bride during the thirteenth century in the company of Marco Polo, the Venetian explorer, and his uncles. The story is told by Marco Polo himself in his immortal work, and he begins by stating that at that time the thoughts of the three Venetians were turning towards home. They had been for seventeen years in the employ of the Great Khan Kubilai, the Mongol conqueror of the Chinese Empire, and during that period they had amassed considerable wealth. The extreme old age of the Khan made them fear that he would die and that his successor would not allow them to depart. They had already applied several times for permission to leave, but the Khan, with whom they were very popular, could not be persuaded to give his consent.

Marco Polo, when this part of his story opens, had just returned from a journey to India. When he arrived at the court of the Khan to make his report, he found that three ambassadors from Persia had reached there before him. They had come to China in search of a wife for their king, Argun, Mongol sovereign of Persia. Argun's wife, the Queen Bologana, had recently died, and in her will she had expressed a desire that her husband should take a second wife from her own clan. Queen Bologana had been, according to the good old nomad custom, first the wife of the father and then of the son Argun, so that when she died on the banks of the Kur in Georgia in April 1286, her last wish assumed something of a nature of a command.

When the three barons from Persia reached the court of the Great Khan they were received with all honour and hospitality by Kulilai, who promised to find them a wife for their king. He sent for the Lady Cocachin, a member of the family of the late queen of Persia, and, as Marco Polo says: 'She was a maiden of seventeen, a very beautiful and charming person.' The three barons declared 'that the lady pleased them well.'

The ambassadors from Persia listened with interest when Marco Polo made his report of his adventures in India, and they conceived the idea of travelling back to their own country in company with the three Venetians, whom they considered 'men of marvellous good sense withal.' Perhaps Marco had helped to direct their thoughts in that direction, because his quick brain realized that this was the opportunity for which he had been waiting. By accompanying the lady to her new home, he would be doing the Khan a service, and at the same time this long journey would provide him with the excuse he needed for terminating his association with the Mongol Emperor and returning to his own home in Venice.

The land route to Persia through Eastern Turkestan was, at that time, exceedingly unsafe. There was fighting in the desert, and therefore it was decided that the journey should be made by sea. The ambassadors were all the more anxious to have the Venetians with them because of Marco's knowledge of the Indian Ocean and of the countries through which the party would have to pass. So they went to the Khan and begged him as a favour to allow the three Latins to go with them.

Kubilai was at first reluctant to give his consent, but once he had done so he did his utmost to help the party depart. He presented the Venetians with two golden tablets of authority which would enable them to travel wherever they wished throughout his domain, and which would procure for them all the necessities they required for their journey. Thirteen ships were equipped, and arrangements were made for a large number of people to accompany the bride. Marco Polo carried with him messages from the Khan to the kings of France, England, and Spain, as well as to other European monarchs.

When all the preparations were completed Marco Polo, his uncles, the three barons, and the Lady Cocachin took leave of the Khan and went on board ship. After three months at sea they arrived at the island of Java, where they remained only long enough to take on provisions and water. Eighteen months later they reached the port, where they disembarked for the last stage overland of their journey to Persia.

It had been an eventful two years at sea. A large percentage of the company died from unknown causes, including two of the barons and one lady in the suite of the bride. The Lady Cocachin was among those who survived the ordeal, but a disappointment awaited her when she reached her destination. During the absence of his ambassadors, Argun, the king, had died. But one Mongol husband was much the same as another and the lady was delivered to Casan, the son of the dead king. Marco ends his account by saying that the lady looked to each of the three Venetians as to a father, and obeyed them as a daughter should, although, he adds, she was young and fair. And when they took leave of her to return to their own country 'she wept for sorrow at the parting.'

This story of four exiled princesses begins and ends with tears, and doubtless many were the tears shed by other royal exiles doomed to a similar fate, who lived and died during the many hundreds of years that passed between the days of the Han dynasty and the time when the Mongol Emperors ruled over China. All these ladies were sisters in misfortune who faced the difficulties and hardships of their new life with courage and fortitude. They seldom complained, although they must all have echoed the sentiments expressed by one of their number, the Lady Hsi-chun, in the following poem:

'Oh that I were a yellow crane
And to my own might fly again.'

VI

WU HOU:
EMPRESS OF THE T'ANG DYNASTY

[625–705 A.D.]

The Master said:

'A plausible tongue and a fascinating expression are seldom associated with true virtue.'

FROM THE DISCOURSES OF CONFUCIUS.
TRANSLATED BY H. A. GILES

Characters in the Story

LI SHIH-MIN

Known as T'ang T'ai Tsung. Second Emperor of the T'ang dynasty

WU CHAO

His concubine. Afterwards known as the Empress Wu

THE EMPEROR KAO TSUNG

Second husband of the Empress Wu

THE EMPEROR CHUNG TSUNG

Son of the Empress Wu by her second husband

THE EMPRESS

First wife of Kao Tsung. Murdered by the Empress Wu

HWAI-YI

A Buddhist priest. Favourite of the Empress Wu

THE EMPRESS WU

FOR three years the wives of the late Emperor T'ang T'ai Tsung had been confined in a Buddhist nunnery. The majority of the ladies had become resigned to their fate. Li.. .n the cloister was preferable to being buried alive as their predecessors had been during the dark ages of antiquity, when custom required that the widows of an Emperor should follow him to the spirit world after his death. Many of the ladies, in gratitude for past and present benefits, became nuns and shaved their heads before taking the vows to serve faithfully the Lord Buddha for the remainder of their days. For women such as these, who had been brought up in the strict code of Confucian morality and trained in obedience since earliest childhood, there was no question of escape, or even of rebellion against the monotony and discomforts of their lives.

Among the many widows of T'ang T'ai Tsung was one who was unable to reconcile herself to a future spent in meditation and prayer as she was still young and beautiful. Her name was Wu Chao, and although of humble birth, her father having been an obscure army official, she had been received into the harem of the Emperor because of her lively intelligence and remarkable learning. She was only fourteen years of age when she entered the palace as a concubine, but already her scholarship had made her a person of some importance, not only within the confines of her own family group, but throughout the province where she lived. Li Shih-min, or the Emperor T'ang T'ai Tsung, as he was called after he ascended the throne as the second Emperor of the T'ang dynasty, enjoyed the society of intellectual women. His new concubine had been chosen for him by his friends, who hoped that she would be able to divert his mind after the death of the Empress, to whom he had been deeply attached. So the girl was admitted to the palace, and was sometimes summoned by the Emperor to recite the classics to him during his rare moments of leisure.

Wu Chao must have felt that all her dreams had come true when she became the concubine of the great Emperor, but she was mistaken. For thirteen years she tried in vain to win his heart. In all probability he regarded her much as her own father had done, as an amusing child endowed with a precocious intellect, but he never loved her, and she remained a concubine only in name. If she had borne him a son she might have been content to renounce the world after his death, but as matters stood she felt that her life was over before it had ever begun. Unsuccessful in the game of love, she had spent those long years in the palace building up for herself a reputation for piety and learning. Her insatiable ambition was hidden behind a cloak of modesty and humility, and no one was allowed to realize that a fierce resentment against her fate burned in the bosom of the quiet and studious concubine.

The success of her duplicity as well as her unimportance during this period of her life can be read in the following words of Fan Hsiao-yu, a writer of the fourteenth century:

'The Emperor T'ai Tsung of the T'angs secretly learned that his issue would be done to death by Wu. He accordingly slew the Wu upon whom his suspicions fell, but the real Wu was all the time at his side.'

The thought never entered the mind of the Emperor that his quiet concubine could ever become a menace to anyone.

After the death of T'ang T'ai Tsung, in the dim obscurity of the cloister, the mind of the former concubine was occupied with ways and means of escape. It was characteristic of her temperament that, although plotting to get away, she should prepare for an alternate path, that of advancement through the church. Therefore with a dramatic gesture of renunciation she took the vows to become a nun. This did not prevent her, when going about her daily tasks, from considering the problem of how to attract the attention of the son of her former husband, the new Emperor Kao Tsung. She knew him for what he was, a weak man easily influenced by others. They had been together on many occasions when his father lay dying. Together they had stood beside the bed of T'ang T'ai Tsung, and Wu Chao had realized that if not the father, at least the son was attracted by her beauty.

How could she arrange to cross the path of the Emperor and remind him of her own existence without breaking any of the rules of tradition and etiquette which governed the behaviour of every member of the court? It would be a difficult task, but this woman had a will of iron and a determination to make the most of every opportunity which fate might offer. In her imagination she was already back in the palace clothed in the robes of the court lady and beloved by a Son of Heaven. Such ideas were as yet only dreams, but Wu Chao was one of those rare women who live to see their dreams come true.

At the end of the three years of mourning the new Emperor Kao Tsung came with his Empress and all the court to offer up sacrifices before the ancestral tablets of his House. The wives of his father were allowed to leave the seclusion of their nunnery in order to be present at the ceremony and among them was Wu Chao. With what care must she have adjusted the head-dress which hid her shaven head and smoothed the folds of her nun's gown. This was the opportunity for which she had been waiting. It might be the only time she would ever be under the same roof with the Emperor and she was determined to make the most of it. The ways and means at her disposal were small, but her determination was great.

During the ceremony, while Kao Tsung was performing the sacrifices and rites required of him, his attention was diverted by the sound of unrestrained sobbing. Among the widows of his father was one who seemed unable to control her grief. Her tears flowed so freely that the Empress also turned to look, and at that moment she saw her husband gaze with recognition and affection at the bowed head of a young woman who appeared to be overcome with emotion. The Empress realized from her husband's expression that he was interested in the young widow, and instead of being jealous she was delighted. Like Wu Chao, she too had a plan and she was searching for a willing tool to help her.

One of the Emperor's concubines was a lady whom his wife feared and hated, and who had lately given birth to a daughter. The Empress herself was childless, therefore she dreaded the growing influence of the young and beautiful mother. She was searching for a counter-attraction: a woman who could lure her husband away from her powerful rival. At the same time the new favourite must remain under her own influence and in no way imperil the position of her patroness at court. As she looked at Wu Chao she thought she had found just the person for whom she had been searching. Who could be better than a woman with a reputation for learning and piety, one who would doubtless serve her faithfully in return for protection?

So it came about that Wu Chao returned to the palace to take her place there as the friend and companion of the childless Empress, in whose apartments she was to live. The hair on her shaven head was allowed to grow, the nun's robe was abandoned for the silken one of her dreams and for the second time fate offered her the opportunity to gratify her ambitions. Now she was determined to succeed and there must have been elation in her heart as she passed through the gates of the palace which she was destined to rule and dominate for the next fifty years.

After her arrival the Emperor was seen more frequently in the apartments of his principal wife. In the company of the Empress he found a talented and witty woman who had many other charms beside those of a pretty face and a graceful figure. As an added attraction she had been his father's wife. In Chinese eyes such a relationship constituted an insurmountable barrier, but there was Tartar blood in Kao Tsung and it was a Tartar custom for the son to marry one of his father's widows. His elder brother had actually reverted to the habits of his nomad ancestors by showing a preference for living in a tent and indulging in activities unsuited to the heir of a great Emperor. As a result he had been banished and disgraced and Kao Tsung had been chosen to take his place. Therefore the Emperor was true to his Tartar blood when he looked at Wu Chao at first with

interest and later with desire. He was a weak man
and she a powerful woman with a will of iron. The
Yang and the Yin principles were reversed in their
case, and, as everyone knows, when this happens
troubles ensue.

As for Wu Chao, she was determined to please and
no word escaped her lips that the Emperor and
Empress did not wish to hear. She entertained them
with her wit and waited upon them with unceasing
devotion. In the course of time, she became the con-
fidante of the Empress and the Emperor spent all his
leisure moments at her side. The self-control which
she had learned during the years she had previously
spent in the palace and her subsequent period of
probation in the nunnery stood her now in good
stead. No hint of her real character was ever allowed
to show itself, and to the court, which was her world,
she appeared the model of all the feminine virtues. In
other words, it seemed as if virtue lived in her heart,
modesty adorned her forehead, sweet speech flowed
from her lips, while work occupied her hands. What
more could any man ask from a beautiful and clever
woman? No wonder the Emperor was charmed.

He encountered opposition, however, when he
proposed to make her his concubine. It was against
all dynastic rules as well as religious principles for a
son to marry his father's former wife, and Kao Tsung
was forced to discuss long and earnestly with his chief
ministers on the subject of the lady's virginity. He
insisted that his father had only considered her in the

light of a rare and precious object of art, to be looked at, admired, and cherished. Even Wu Chao herself appeared doubtful:

'Although I never shared the bed of your father,' she said, 'I was given the title of concubine. Is it permissible that I should belong to you? You must reflect on both sides of the question before you acquaint your slave with your decision.'

Opposition only strengthened the resolve of the Emperor, who was stubborn as well as weak, and he informed his ministers that he was about to take Wu Chao into his harem. The Empress supported her husband, a fact which carried great weight in an affair of this kind, and in the end Wu Chao became an imperial concubine for the second time. The people considered the union incestuous and murmured against her, but there was no open revolt, although soon after her elevation in rank a disastrous flood occurred. Water has a feminine significance to the Chinese people, and it was said that Heaven was displeased.

Up to this period of her career the ambitions of Wu Chao had been achieved without harm to others. As a woman of little importance and without a powerful protector devoted to her interests she had been obliged to mask her true feelings. Now all was changed. Secure in the affections of the Emperor she was prepared to strike her first blow. She intended to be Empress and nothing, not even the life of her own child, would be allowed to stand in her way.

If her first child had been a son she might have achieved her aim without resort to murder, because the position of the mother of the Emperor's only son would have been a powerful one. But the child proved to be a girl and Wu Chao determined to sacrifice it. Soon after its birth the Empress came to visit her friend. She took the babe in her arms and caressed it before returning it to its cradle. Then she left the room followed by all the attendants. When she was alone Wu Chao leapt from her bed, and before her waiting-women returned she had strangled the infant with her own hands. No one noticed anything as the child appeared to be asleep.

The Emperor found his infant daughter dead when he came to visit the mother and to congratulate her on the happy event. Wu Chao appeared distraught with grief, and between her sobs hinted darkly that jealousy had been the motive for the deed. The Empress had been the last person to see the child alive, therefore it was not difficult to suggest that she had murdered it. The Emperor knew his wife to be a kind-hearted woman, beloved and respected by all, but suspicion was so cleverly planted in his mind that he believed what Wu Chao wanted him to believe. Even so he was not prepared to publicly accuse the Empress of such a fantastic crime. She came from a noble family and had powerful connections and friends. A suspicion would not be considered sufficient reason to depose her and some other excuse must be found.

Wu Chao realized that further steps must be taken before she could realize her ambition and so she set about to undermine the positions of all those who, for one reason or another, were strongest in their support of the Empress. Reports concerning these people were brought to her by her eunuch spies, and when placed before the Emperor she interpreted them in such a way that he believed anything she said. Soon many of the nobles, even those remotely connected with the family of the Empress, found themselves deprived of their positions, while their places at court were taken by relatives and friends of the concubine. In this way Wu Chao built up her own party and surrounded herself with men who owed their advancement to her efforts.

Kao Tsung wished to govern alone, as his father had done before him, but having none of the genius of T'ang T'ai Tsung he needed to have someone near him who was able to make his decisions for him and who could explain those matters which his own intelligence was unable to grasp. Wu Chao, with her clear, lucid mind and her knowledge of history, appeared to him to be the only person capable of unravelling complicated affairs. Soon she became the oracle which he consulted on every occasion. So indispensable did he find her that it was only one step further to have her present at all audiences. At first she remained quietly seated behind a curtain, only spitting or coughing occasionally to make sure that her presence was not forgotten, but later the curtain was pushed back sufficiently to allow her to take part in the discussions.

This active intervention in state affairs did not add to the popularity of the concubine with the ministers of the Crown, and when the Emperor at length proposed to remove the Empress from her high position because of her sterility, the nobles and mandarins were united in their opposition. The consent of the highest tribunal in the land was necessary and all the greatest personages in the Empire were against the change. One counsellor, bolder than the rest, said:

'If your Majesty for particular reasons with which you do not wish to acquaint us, wishes absolutely to give us another Empress in the place of the one we honour today, so be it. But, Sire, it must not be the Princess Wu Chao. They say throughout the Empire that she was one of your father's wives. The sublime rank to which you wish to raise her would bring to the attention of everyone a fact which all wish to ignore.'

The Emperor contented himself with ordering the minister to leave the palace, but Wu Chao, who had been, as usual, hidden behind her curtain, was furious and could no longer restrain herself. She cried out that the minister deserved punishment for his presumption and should be cut to pieces. Only the intercession of the other nobles saved the life of the offender and the meeting broke up without any decision having been reached.

It is possible that the Emperor would have been afraid to carry out his plan in the face of so much opposition had not Wu Chao been at his side to remind him that among all those who had spoken against her there had been no representative of the army. If the troops were not hostile to the change no trouble could be serious enough to cause alarm. The commander of the army was then consulted, and as this man did not consider the affair important and knew nothing of the ambitions of Wu Chao, he told the Emperor that, as far as he was concerned, it did not matter who was made Empress. If a revolt occurred he would see to it that order was maintained.

The support of the army was all that Kao Tsung needed and he no longer hesitated to give the order to depose the Empress. She was imprisoned with the pretty concubine who had pleased him in former days in a distant part of the palace, and Wu Chao was proclaimed Empress. Wu Hou was the title which she received at the time of her elevation in rank, and as Wu Hou she is known to posterity.

The Emperor, although he had agreed to the disgrace and imprisonment of his two former wives, still retained a certain affection for them, and one day he was unwise enough to visit them secretly in order to assure them that their confinement would not be a long one. Wu Hou, who was informed of his visit by her spies, was furious. She said nothing at the time but waited until the Emperor, who suffered from epilepsy, was seized by one of his periodical attacks, which deprived him of his faculties for the time being. When this happened she sent two of her eunuchs to the prison where the ladies were confined with orders to cut off their legs and arms.

There are various accounts of the terrible sufferings which these unfortunate women endured for twenty-four hours before they died, and one report states that Wu Hou pickled the severed arms and legs of her victims in wine and said she was making a stew for her enemies. She had the audacity to announce their deaths to the Emperor herself, but the unfortunate Kao Tsung was by this time so completely under her domination that he not even dared to protest. After this double murder Wu Hou often thought she saw the ghosts of the two women with streaming hair and blood flowing from their wounds. To get away from such an unpleasant apparition she rebuilt the palace at Loyang and moved the capital to that city from Ch'ang-an.

The ministers who had spoken against the change were silent as there was nothing more they could do. The former Empress was now dead and Wu Hou reigned in her place. Although they retained their posts and remained in possession of their honours and titles, they were not forgotten by the new Empress. She regarded them as victims who, at some future date, must of necessity be sacrificed to her ambition.

That they had spoken against her was sufficient reason for their death-warrant to be sent to them when the occasion should present itself. She never forgot an insult, but neither was she in a hurry to carry out her vengeance. The blow was always dealt with every appearance of justice behind it, and the victim was usually allowed to enjoy a false sense of security for a period of time. It was as if contemplating a murder gave her pleasure, especially when the victim was one who had offended her vanity.

The vanity of Wu Hou was colossal. At the height of her power, instead of allowing herself to be compared to a rose or a lily, the rose and the lily were compared to her, and men were forced to say that a certain flower was as beautiful as their Empress. Like so many other rulers she cherished the illusion of her own divinity, and the title of 'Celestial,' which she was later to receive, was an outward expression of an inner conviction. Only a woman labouring under such a delusion could command the peonies to bloom on a certain day, and when they failed to respond order their heads to be chopped off and their roots torn from the ground. Actions such as this one contained an element of the ridiculous, but Wu Hou was enough of a statesman to counteract their obvious effect by some concession to public opinion. She was quick to detect the slightest hint of ridicule on the part of others, and punished jokes with the greatest severity.

At one time one of the brothers of the Emperor

committed the indiscretion of writing, with the help of a famous scholar, an allegory about a hen. Wu Hou obtained a copy of the poem, which had caused much laughter in court circles, and at once identified herself with the hen. This was an insult not to be endured and she induced her husband to exile his brother. She feared the sharp tongue and biting wit of the scholar, and when she contemplated taking a step which she knew the *literati* would consider extravagant, she would bribe them with positions at court, or in some other way distract their attention from herself. When she was ready to assume the title of 'Celestial' she called them all to the palace and set them to work on the dynastic history of the late Sui and early T'ang times, an honour they much coveted.

Her aim was always to propitiate the scholars because she appreciated the literary ability of others and objected only to their wit when it was directed against herself. She was the first Chinese ruler to make poetry a requisite in examinations for degrees and an important course leading to official promotion. During this paradoxical reign when blood flowed freely and murder was a daily occurrence, every statesman was obliged to be a poet as well as a courtier. It is possible that the gentle art of verse-making suffered from official regulations, as the great poets who sang of the fame of the T'ang dynasty lived and flourished during the reigns of the successors of the Empress Wu, when life was easier and grim terror had ceased to stalk through the palace.

The family life of the Empress went on behind the
screen of high politics like that of any other woman,
and her children were born with an almost monotonous regularity. Four sons and one daughter are
known to have survived their childhood, and there
may have been others whose names are not recorded.
When her own position was assured, Wu Hou turned
her attention to that of her eldest son, a child of four
years of age, whom she wished to appoint as heir to
the throne. There was already an Heir Apparent, the
adopted son of the late Empress, but Wu Hou, in
spite of opposition, managed by means of intrigue to
cause his disgrace and have her own son put in his
place. During the ceremonies prescribed for this
event no one present showed any joy. Neither bribes
nor flattery were sufficient to remove the marks of
gloom from the faces of those present. Sobs and
weeping were heard as was customary at a funeral.
There is always the element of self-pity in excessive
expressions of grief, and the princes and nobles who
shed tears that day may have had a premonition of
what was to come. Their sobs were for themselves
as well as for the exiled prince, and many must have
realized that sooner or later they too would be sent
into exile, or perhaps even to their death. Their
forebodings were only too well justified, as few who
were present at the ceremony escaped the vengeance
of the Empress.

She had two favourite methods for ridding herself
of the people who stood in her way. One was to

create an imaginary plot which would convince the Emperor that the man she wished to remove was guilty of treason against the state. The other was more subtle. She would promote the unfortunate person to a position for which he was unfitted and where he could not help making mistakes. Then she would make much of his mistakes, and it was easy for her to say that such a man was incapable of holding any post at all and should be punished. Those deprived of their positions and wealth suffered great hardships. Tu Fu, the poet, who lived during the reign of the grandson of the Empress Wu, has told us in his poems all about the fate of the penniless exiles. Day by day he describes his sufferings after he himself had received the same sentence. He was the spokesman, as it were, of all those who lost everything because of imperial displeasure. On his journey away from the court after his banishment, he writes:

'*My life is bitter, tossed as by waves I am a vagrant;*
When can I finally reach an ending?'

And again another poem he says:

'*My body is like a drifting cloud,*
Shall it be driven South or North?'

The children of the Empress were no more immune from her displeasure than the humblest of her subjects. Four sons succeeded each other as Heir

Apparent, each one being removed when he began to differ with his imperious mother. The health of the Emperor, which continued to decline during the years of his marriage, gave Wu Hou the excuse she needed to assume supreme control of the state, and neither the care of a large family nor the indisposition of her husband were ever allowed to interfere with her public duties. It was her habit to arrive at the hall of audience in the early dawn while others in the palace were still asleep, and her capacity for hard work was the despair of those who served her. Neither her sons nor her ministers were allowed to oppose her, and as for her husband, the Emperor, he had long ago given up any such attempt.

It is probable that only a very ill man or one who was very weak would have submitted to the domination of a woman like Wu Hou. Kao Tsung was both, and he was completely at the mercy of his powerful wife. Very often she would compel him to travel with her about the country because a change of scene amused her. At one time she insisted that he worship first at the tomb of Confucius and then at that of L'ao Tzu, while Buddha was not forgotten. A colossal image of Amitaba Buddha was built in one of the cave temples at Yun-Kang by order of the Empress, who used for its construction a portion of the money allowed her by the state to buy cosmetics. In this way she kept on good terms with the three great religions of her country and used them impartially for her own advantage.

On one of these trips with the Emperor, Wu Hou fulfilled her heart's desire. She worshipped the Powers of Heaven and Earth with all the observances that hitherto had been the exclusive right of an emperor. The ceremony took place on the top of a mountain, where the unfortunate Kao Tsung, in spite of his illness, was required to go through a long and tiring ritual. To protect him from the wind and rain a small rush-covered hut had been constructed, as was customary. As soon as Kao Tsung had performed his part, he and his ministers hurried away. He had given his consent to the sacrilege which was to follow but he did not wish to witness it.

When he had gone a hurried change of scene took place. The simple hut was replaced by a brilliantly coloured silk tent with curtains of gorgeous brocade, and Wu Hou, surrounded by her ladies and the eunuchs of the court, took her husband's place before the altar. The customary slab of rock on which the Emperor had knelt was now covered with the softest cushions so that the knees of the Celestial Empress, as she called herself, would not come in contact with the hard stone. This was the apex of her career. Her vanity was satisfied and she could afford to be generous. The people were horrified by the sacrilege, but to appease them a general amnesty was conceded, no tribute was demanded for the space of one year, and every official was raised a step in rank. No wonder that nothing was said about the behaviour of a woman who never forgot that the crowd, which was always watching her, needed diversion.

Even the Jesuit historians, writing about her centuries later with outraged feelings, record that she was a magnificent administrator:

'It seems to me,' says Père Amyiot, 'that to account for all the contradictions in the life of this Princess that she must have possessed a superior intelligence and a profound insight into political affairs. She offended every propriety and yet brought to their successful conclusions many projects which had seemed impossible; she was cruel and ruthless to the last degree and yet the people lived out their lives in tranquillity and very little opposition to her despotic power ever raised its head.'

One is inclined to compare her to a great conqueror such as Genghis Khan, who was able to subdue whole cities with a handful of men. Like him, she must have been inspired with the belief in her own infallibility.

To understand the way in which Wu Hou treated her own sons, it is necessary to realize that in her eyes they belonged to the house of T'ang, and like the Empress Lu of the Han dynasty, she had secretly determined to destroy her husband's House and replace it by her own. It was the fate of the poor epileptic Emperor to have his race and his family despised by the wife he himself had failed to subdue. He had raised her to the highest position in the state and had given her honours that no woman before her had ever received, but Wu Hou was a woman who did not appreciate kindness and who only respected force. At the end of her life, when she was over eighty years of age, it took a small army to subdue her, and until that time no organized resistance to her rule ever had a chance of success.

Her eldest son, who had been made Heir Apparent at the early age of four, grew into a wise and good man, too good and too wise to please his autocratic mother. One day he interceded for the daughters of the concubine who had perished at the same time as the former Empress. The girls, he said, were at an age to marry, and suitable husbands should be found for them. His mother agreed to his request, but the husbands she considered suitable were two men serving in the palace guard. They were chosen at random from amongst those of the lowest rank, and each was presented with an imperial princess. A few days later the prince died suddenly. Until that time he had been in the best of health and no one knew of any illness which might have caused his sudden death.

The second son then took his place and applied himself to the task of learning the ways of government, as the approaching death of his father made it seem probable that he would soon be called to the throne. Again the Empress was displeased, as she thought that such determination might foreshadow a waning of her own power, and so he was accused of being concerned in the assassination of one of the ministers of the state. The palace of the Heir Apparent was searched, and some horses and arms were found which proved sufficient evidence of treasonable intentions to have him removed and imprisoned. The youth spent the remainder of his life moving from prison to prison, as his mother considered it dangerous to leave him long in the same spot. Eventually he was advised to commit suicide in order to escape from a disgraceful death.

The Emperor Kao made a last feeble effort to save the lives of the remainder of his family by discussing with one of his ministers the possibilities of deposing Wu Hou. The conversation was reported to the Empress by a spy and, descending upon her husband like a fury, she demanded an explanation. The Emperor was too weak to stand up for himself, so he blamed the minister for suggesting such a plan. Needless to say, the minister lost both his post and his head, and from that time until his death the Emperor was never allowed to receive anyone in audience alone. He became almost blind and quite incapable of any effort before he died in A.D. 683. When he felt his end approaching, he sent for his ministers and dictated the following edict:

'I leave the Empire to the son that I have named Heir Apparent, but it is my wish that he consults with the Empress his mother, and that he does nothing without her consent.'

After the death of his father, the third son of Wu Hou was proclaimed Emperor under the title of Chung Tsung. His hands had been tied by his father's orders, and after reigning only two months an indiscreet remark, said in a moment of anger, was reported to the Empress, who used it as the excuse for deposing him. She was now the undisputed master of the state. Her fourth son was given the title of Emperor, but as he and his family were virtually prisoners in the palace it was a purely nominal position. This fourth son was the father of Ming Huang, the 'Bright Emperor' of the T'ang dynasty, who fought his way to the throne after his father and uncle had both died. Chung Tsung, the legitimate Emperor, remained in imprisonment or exile for over twenty years, until the army revolted and restored him to the throne after his spirit had been broken and his days were numbered. All the sons of the Empress Wu lived their lives in an atmosphere of intrigue and unrest and it was left to her grandson to inaugurate a new era when art was to take the place of murder—for a while—and when beauty was to reign triumphant, the undisputed mistress of the new court.

Among the many crimes of which the Empress Wu was accused was that of practising the art of magic. Not long before the death of her husband, the

Emperor, a Taoist priest, noted for his proficiency in the black arts, was secretly introduced into the palace. This man was reported to possess the most surprising powers, and the court feared the influence which he came to exert over the Empress. She gave him complete freedom to go or come as he pleased and for hours she would remain closeted with him privately. Such conduct would of necessity give rise to much adverse comment, and Wu Hou was severely criticized for her intimacy with the priest.

He was only the first, however, of a succession of Taoist or Buddhist priests with whom the Empress was on intimate terms and there are various explanations of what might otherwise appear to be a series of casual love affairs. One such explanation is that Wu Hou was searching for the elixir of life, a favourite pastime with rulers of the Chinese world since the early days of the Han dynasty. A woman like the Empress, who was vain enough to believe in her own divinity, might easily go one step further and indulge in dreams of everlasting life on earth. Or, it is equally possible, that she hoped to use magic as an instrument of vengeance and wished to learn new and subtle means of disposing of her enemies.

The Jesuits, in their history of China, give an even simpler explanation which is quite plausible. They suggest that she used the priests as spies and that she received reports from them every night. This theory is based on the fact that she had what we would call a spy mania. Her spies were everywhere and nothing could take place without her knowledge. Such excessive precautions could only have seemed necessary to one who was troubled with a deep, subconscious sense of insecurity. Fear, and the bitter realization in moments of lucidity that her own inferior birth placed her beneath those people whom she was endeavouring to destroy, may have been responsible for her exaggerated precautions and unnecessary cruelties.

Her spy mania was responsible for the institution of a custom which was followed in later centuries by the Doges of Venice. Wu Hou did not invent the Lion's Mouth, but she had a large iron box made with a slip through which anonymous letters could be inserted. The key was kept in her own apartments, where every night the box was brought for her to open. She requested the people to report to her through this medium anything about the conduct of those in high places which would be of interest to her, and false accusations and personal spite were given imperial sanction. The Empress was far too clever not to be aware of what she was doing, but her box remained in operation until hosts of people had perished and scarcely a family of note in the Empire was not wearing mourning. Then, when her vengeance was satisfied, she allowed herself to be persuaded that such proceedings were not for the permanent good of the state, and a second edict was issued stating that in future all communications must be signed and that those writers who could not prove their accusations would be punished by death. Many hundreds of people perished as the result of the second edict alone.

The most famous of the priest-confidants of the Empress was a man named Hwai-yi. To please him she built a magnificent temple and appointed him abbot with ten thousand Buddhist priests directly under his orders. But for once the Empress had made a mistake. It was pointed out to her that ten thousand men gathered together who, from their looks, had obviously not been chosen for their piety but for their youth and strength, might easily become a menace to the state. The Empress realized the truth of this observation and immediately gave orders for the priests to be dispersed and banished to different parts of the Empire. Hwai-yi was furious and in revenge burned the temple to the ground. But the Empress knew when to strike and when it was best to remain silent and this time her only retaliation was to order the temple to be rebuilt.

Some time later, perhaps when she had learned from her priest all that she thought he was able to teach her, she made him a general and gave him the command of a large army which had been raised to fight against the Turks. With such a commander the campaign was doomed in the beginning, and when the priest had clearly demonstrated his lack of ability in the art of war, Wu Hou was provided with the excuse she needed to have him put to death. This device of placing a man in a position which he was unable to fill with honour was a favourite one with the Empress.

If her priest had been a student of history he might
have escaped the scaffold had he remembered the wise
words of the philosopher Chuang Tzu, who, when
asked to take office by the Prince of Ch'u, refused,
saying that it was better to be a live tortoise wagging
its tail in the mud than to be the sacred one, dead
these three thousand years, which the prince kept in
a box on his ancestral shrine.

The House of T'ang was throughout the reign of
the Empress Wu the object of her hatred and
vengeance. At one time several of the princes belong-
ing to her husband's family, finding their positions
and lands slipping away from them, decided to revolt.
The uprising was unsuccessful owing to the fact that
the leaders could not agree among themselves, but
Wu Hou used it as an excuse to break their power.
Over five thousand people connected with that House,
either as relatives, servants, or friends, were banished
to distant parts of the Empire while the ringleaders
of the revolt were executed.

While pursuing her attempt to destroy the House
of T'ang, the Empress never forgot her plan, which
was to found a dynasty of her own. She considered it
necessary to create for herself an imaginary line of
royal ancestors, so her father was given the posthumous title of Emperor and her grandfather and other
ancestors accorded high rank. Seven great halls were
erected for appropriate ceremonies of worship, and
the ritual she used on these occasions was that of the
great Chou dynasty. It was her wish to change the

name of the dynasty to that of Chou, and to name one
of her nephews as her successor in place of her own son.

It is surprising that after so many years of despotic
rule and the fall of so many men who opposed her
policies, there should still remain those brave enough
to attempt to restrain her from committing follies
which would endanger the peace of the country.
This time a minister had sufficient courage to remind
her of the debt which she owed to her husband's clan
and how poorly she would repay it if she took the
step which she contemplated. He assured her that the
result would be civil war and the ultimate destruction
of her own family. What finally decided her were his
last words, apparently spoken at random as he left the
audience.

'Do you believe,' he said, 'that your nephew
whom you wish to make Emperor will have proper
respect for you after your death? You may be sure
that he will give preference to his own father and
mother. They will be raised to the rank of Emperor
and Empress and their names will be written first
in the hall of the ancestors. You will be fortunate
if your tablet is left on one side.'

The other ministers who were consulted all agreed
with the first and each one expressed a desire for the
recall of the legitimate Emperor Chung Tsung, saying
that the wishes of the entire nation could not be
ignored.

In the end the Empress gave in and recalled her son from exile, stating in an edict that during his years of imprisonment his conduct had been beyond reproach and that she now considered him worthy to return to her side for instruction in government matters. She made the mistake, however, of wishing to have the Emperor renounce the name of Li, which was that of the House of T'ang, and adopt her own name of Wu, thus showing that she still clung to the idea of obliterating the name of the reigning dynasty.

Soon after the return of Chung Tsung, the Empress had an unpleasant surprise. She had given her son the command of an army about to march against the Tartars, but she had not foreseen that the whole nation would show its joy at his return by sending men from every part of the Empire to serve under him. Such a display of devotion alarmed Wu Hou, and she refused to allow her son to leave the capital, giving as an excuse that the fatigue of the campaign would endanger his delicate health. The Emperor, who had learned the futility of opposing his mother, agreed to all her demands. Like his father before him, he was a weak man, first dominated by his mother, and later by his wife, who, incidentally, attempted to follow in the footsteps of her mother-in-law.

Perhaps it was because she had had her own way long enough, or perhaps it was only because she was growing old, but whatever the cause, the Empress became careless, and in the end it was an error of judgment which caused her downfall. She had taken into her confidence two young nobles by the name of Tchang, who misused the powerful position which they enjoyed and became excessively proud and over-bearing. They boasted of state secrets told them by the Empress and in other ways betrayed their patron and protector. As they had made many enemies among the other courtiers there were those only too ready to believe that the Empress conspired with them in order to resurrect her old plan of placing her nephew on the throne.

One of her counsellors told Wu Hou that she was endangering the throne by allowing these men to go in and out of the palace as they chose, and he added that it was possible they abused her confidence. The minister already had sufficient evidence to have the brothers Tchang executed, but he wished to arrange matters so that the request for their arrest was made through the court of punishments. Eventually the Empress was obliged to send both men to prison in order to clear herself of the suspicion of conspiring against her own son, but the day after their arrest they returned in triumph to the palace, as if com-pletely exonerated from any charge made against them.

Such a travesty of justice sincerely shocked the president of the court of punishments, and he now believed that the Empress was plotting with the brothers to remove the Emperor Chung Tsung. He secretly approached the general in command of the army and several of the most important nobles and secured their co-operation in a plot to save the throne for the Emperor and at the same time remove Wu Hou from the position of power which she had enjoyed for such a long time. Other conspiracies during the reign of the Empress had failed and the only possible explanation of the success of this one is that old age had made her careless and that she no longer had the foresight and grasp of affairs which she had previously possessed. A handful of men, headed by her son, the Emperor, were able to force their way into the palace and kill the brothers Tchang at her feet.

We can but admire the Empress Wu as she stood on the steps of the throne, looking first at the son who had defied her and then at the dead bodies of the two young men. With the same air of authority with which she usually issued her orders, she addressed the Emperor:

'You came,' she said, 'to massacre the two men you hated. There they are—dead. Go away and take these people with you.'

The Emperor might have hesitated. Years of imprisonment had destroyed his spirit, but one of the nobles intervened before Chung Tsung had a chance to reply:

''To what place,' he asked, 'do you wish the Emperor to retire? He is in his own palace and for many years he has been of an age to reign. There is nothing for you to do, Madam, but to turn over the government to him. The time has come for you to comply with his wishes.'

The old Empress realized that her day was over, and she obeyed the order with good grace. She escorted her son to the throne on which she had sat for so many long years, turned over to him the seals of office, and then retired to a palace reserved for the ladies of the court. Her reign had come to an end and there was no longer any reason for her to live. Soon afterwards, at the age of eighty-two, she died, unloved and unmourned, but her son, who for twenty-two years had been her victim, had the magnanimity to confirm his mother in the last title which she chose her herself. Vain to the end, Wu Hou wished to be known to posterity by the title of 'One designated by Heaven to reign over men.'

The personality of this extraordinary woman is so full of contradictions that it is difficult to draw conclusions. There was the woman of letters, who added new characters to the complicated Chinese script. There was the great ruler, who protected her people and made it possible for them to live and work in peace. And yet, on the other hand, we find the twin monsters of cruelty and pride dominating her character. We can picture her arriving in the early dawn at the hall of audience, ready to begin her work for the day, and we can see her closeted late at night with a disreputable, discredited priest poring over books of magic. But whether she was performing religious ceremonies in an Emperor's robes, or whether she was only addressing her own court, she was always mistress of the situation. What was the secret of her success? Perhaps it was her immense vitality, which, when added to a personality of unusual strength, is bound to leave its mark on history.

The Lady Yang Kuei-fei

VII

THE BELOVED OF AN EMPEROR:
YANG KUEI-FEI

[DIED 756 A.D.]

'What matter if the snow
Blot out the garden? She shall still recline
Upon the scented balustrade and glow
With spring that thrills her warm blood into wine.'

FROM 'AN EMPEROR'S LOVE,' BY
LI T'AI-PO. RENDERED INTO
ENGLISH BY L. CRAMNER-BYNG

Characters in the Story

THE EMPEROR MING HUANG	The 'Bright Emperor' of the T'ang dynasty
YANG KUEI-FEI	His favourite concubine
YANG HAN KUO YANG KUO KUO YANG CH'IN KUO	} Her three sisters
YANG KUO-CHUNG	The Prime Minister
AN LU-SHAN	A Turkish general who revolted against the Emperor
PRINCE LOYALTY	The Heir Apparent
KO-SHU HAN	A General
KAO LI-SHIH	Chief Eunuch
LI T'AI-PO	A famous poet
TU FU	Another famous poet
WU TAO-TZU	A famous painter

THE BELOVED OF AN EMPEROR

THERE are no poets today to immortalize beautiful women as Li T'ai-po and Tu Fu immortalized Yang Kuei-fei. When we read their songs we seem to see her before us, as they saw her, an ever-living symbol of eternal spring. Like that old man, the Emperor, who doted on her and to whom she was the light of the sun, we sit at her feet today as in the presence of one of the world's great masterpieces. She was a masterpiece. One that lived and breathed twelve hundred years ago. But to love her was to court destruction and she brought ruin to the old Emperor and all his house. She and others of her clan destroyed the work of valiant men and when she died she left her country prostrate beneath the feet of the invader. The heroine of many dramas and the inspiration of countless poems, Yang Kuei-fei takes her place in history as one of the most beautiful as well as one of the most destructive women of all times.

The Chinese have a proverb: 'When Yang is in the ascendant, Yin is born,' which means, translated into our language, that when a man has devoted the better part of his life to the ordinary business of living, the

Yin, or emotional side of his nature, rises to the surface and demands its rights. When such a period occurs, all that which has formerly seemed important loses its significance. The will-of-the-wisp of illusion leads the man hither and thither, taking him on strange and complicated deviations from his former path in life. Ming Huang, the 'Bright Emperor' of the T'ang dynasty, was an example of the profound truth of this theory. From the moment he saw Yang Kuei-fei bathing in the lake near his palace in the Li Mountains, he was destined to sit at her feet, learning from her the emotional mysteries of what the Chinese call Yin.

The reign of Ming Huang had begun with great promise. Such great promise, in fact, that if he had only died before that fateful day, he would have been considered by posterity as one of the most competent Sons of Heaven who ever sat upon the throne of China. His tireless energy may have been inherited from his grandmother, the famous Empress Wu, and he was able to use it constructively for the good of his country. If he had a fault it was that of devoting too much time to the 'Pear Garden,' a school which he established for the purpose of teaching music to students of both sexes.

The story runs that the school was the direct result of a visit paid to the moon by the Emperor in the company of a magician. During this unusual expedition he was allowed to witness a miraculous performance of singing and dancing given by moon-maidens of surpassing loveliness. So impressed was he that upon his return to earth he organized the famous body of operatic artists known as the Pear Garden Performers. Many other schools of a less spectacular origin were founded by this good and great Emperor, including the Han Lin Academy, an institution of learning which existed until the present century.

Not only education, but reforms occupied him in his younger days. Luxury was discouraged, and for a time the silk factories were closed, while the ladies of the court were deprived of their jewels and forbidden to wear embroidered gowns. Like his ancestor, the Emperor T'ang T'ai Tsung, founder of the dynasty, he must have realized that the excessive luxury of the Chinese court was bad for a hardy northern race like the T'ang, and he attempted to break away from it, though with a conspicuous lack of success. But the temperament of the poet combined with the impracticable vision of the dreamer proved in the end to be the undoing of the Emperor. His love of beauty made him peculiarly susceptible to human loveliness, and after one glance at Yang Kuei-fei his plans for reform were forgotten. In a twinkling of an eye even the memory of his journey to the moon took second place.

The Emperor's capital was at Ch'ang-an, but twenty-five miles outside the city, in the heart of the Li Mountains, he had a summer palace which he called the Palace of Glorious Purity. T'ang T'ai Tsung had been the original builder of the palace, which was situated in a landscape of rare natural beauty. Hot springs, which gushed out of the mountain, had been diverted so as to flow into an artificial lake, around the shores of which shrubs and trees had been planted. In the middle of the lake, floating on the face of the water like colourful aquatic plants, were small pavilions of exquisite design and workmanship, roofed with brilliantly coloured tiles. Here the Emperor could rest from the cares of his busy life and discuss poetry and art with the men of genius who flocked to his court, while all the time his beloved orchestra played soft music on the shore.

It is even possible that on the fatal day when Yang Kuei-fei came to the lake to bathe the Emperor was sitting alone, meditating, as was his custom, on the Immortals of the Taoist Heaven. She wore, we are told, a cloak of embroidered gauze through which her naked body shone with a wonderful light, and he may have thought, while her maids removed the cloak, that a Hsien, a supernatural being, had come to earth to be his guest.

We can almost see her as she stood there, poised on the bank, her dainty feet testing the warmth of the water before abandoning her body to its embrace, while her hair, like a lustrous dark cloud, floated behind her. Words between the two—the Emperor half concealed in his pavilion and the girl on the shore—were not necessary. Yang Kuei-fei was not one of those women who sway empires through words or deeds. She was ever a passive instrument of

destiny. Men only had to look at her to be transformed, as Ming Huang was transformed when he
forgot his country and his honour for her sake. From
that moment he lived only to possess her.

A contemporary poet has described this fateful
meeting:

> 'The Waters of Hua'ch'ing beheld her stand,
> Laving her body in the crystal wave,
> Whose dimpled fount a warmth perennial gave.
> Then when, her girls attending, forth she came,·
> A reed in motion and a rose in flame,
> An empire passed into a maid's control,
> And with her eyes she won a monarch's soul.'

To the poets she was the eternal goddess of spring.
Her body, they said, exuded a curious fragrance, so
that she needed no other perfume than her own to
intoxicate the senses of those about her. She had
eyebrows curved like willow blossoms, and jasmine
flowers were compared to her teeth. Even her complexion was so perfect that rouge or powder marred
its beauty, and among the painted ladies of the court
she alone dared to ignore convention and remain as
nature made her. Not only in the matter of paint and
powder was Kuei-fei a capricious beauty, but in other
ways as well. Secure in the knowledge of her own
unequalled charms, she felt free to follow the dictates
of her fancy.

Exceptional women were free under the T'ang

dynasty to do as they pleased. The sister of the Emperor T'ang T'ai Tsung had sold her jewels to raise an army, and had fought beside her brother against the forces of the Sui Emperor. The wife of the son of the great Emperor, the famous Empress Wu, had defied criticism when she usurped the privileges of her husband and sons; while two generations later, during the reign of Ming Huang, the sisters of Kuei-fei galloped over the countryside on their horses, and their lovers and their lack of decorum caused bitter adverse comment. The women got out of hand during the T'ang. They ceased to listen to the wise words of Confucius and it is possible that the tiny bound feet, the 'golden lilies,' of the Chinese women, were a subtle revenge on the part of their husbands to bring them back to the path of virtue. Crippled feet, which were to be their heritage for over a thousand years, although considered a refinement of beauty, were an effective substitute for the 'Purdah' of other Eastern lands.

Even an Emperor sometimes has a desire that is difficult or even impossible to gratify, and in this case Yang Kuei-fei was the concubine of Ming Huang's eighteenth son, Prince Shou, whose name means Longevity. This would have been an inappropriate title had his early death been required in order to enable the Emperor to obtain Kuei-fei, but fortunately no such expedient was necessary and the transfer of the girl from the harem of the son to that of the father was accomplished without bloodshed. It may have been thought that a period of purification was necessary so she was sent for a time to a Taoist nunnery, where doubtless she was instructed in all the secrets of that strange and mysterious religion.

It seems probable that the introduction of Yang Kuei-fei into the court was an attempt on the part of the Taoist priesthood to obtain control over the Emperor. The legend of his journey to the moon before he met her is highly symbolic and seems to suggest that the Emperor himself had been initiated into the Taoist mysteries; that is, at one time or another he had been made aware of the knowledge both exoteric and esoteric which the Taoists claim as their own, and which was and still is supposed to contain the true secrets of the universe. In Taoist mythology a journey to the moon has always meant that the initiate has reached the 'lunar state,' which is the state of supreme awareness, and that he has become master of all knowledge. The presence at his side of a woman, who had received instruction of a similar nature and who could use her great influence with the Emperor to lead him into paths prescribed by the Taoist priests, would have given them a firm foothold at court and enabled them to influence the future policies of the dynasty.

Nothing is left to chance in a highly complicated and ritualistic court like that of the Chinese emperors, and it is possible that some powerful influence arranged what appeared on the surface to be a chance meeting between the Emperor and Kuei-fei. That the

Taoists looked on complacently while this unusual transfer of a wife from her husband to her father-in-law took place is more or less proved by contemporary gossip, which credits the Emperor with nightly visits to his love during her period of seclusion in the nunnery.

To reconstruct the court life of the eighth century over which Kuei-fei reigned as queen as soon as Ming Huang was able to publicly claim her as his own, it is necessary to turn to Japan, for the Japanese adopted the culture of the T'ang and transplanted it to their own country, where it has remained ever since as the model of all that is desirable on earth. Even the lovely kimonos of the Japanese women are modelled after the robes worn by Kuei-fei and her sisters. During the age of the T'ang, the sons of Japanese nobles were sent to Ch'ang-an to study as they are sent to London or New York today. Afterwards they would return to their own country and attempt to reproduce, with that minute attention to detail for which the Japanese are famous, an alien civilization in their own land.

An allusion to the fact that Japan owed her culture and civilization to China is contained in the following poem, written impromptu by a Japanese envoy for one of the Ming emperors. The Japanese could write beautiful Chinese characters, but they were unable to speak the language, so that when the Emperor questioned the envoy about the manners and customs of his country, he received in reply a poem.

'Our country, Sire, in much like yours;
Our men are like your men of old;
Our hats and coats we took from you,
Rites too, and music, so I'm told.
In silver jars we store our wine;
We cut our food with golden knives;
And every year in early spring
The peach and plum adorn our lives.

We immediately think of Japan when we read about the gardens of the Emperor's palace at Ch'ang-an. As in Japan, little streams wandered in and out among the flowers and came to an end in a bathing pool or a fish pond. Carved stone bridges crossed the streams at intervals, while on the lake brightly painted boats in the shape of dragons waited to row the guests to small islands, where they would find pavilions hung with bells that tinkled in the breeze.

On fête days the gardens and terraces were lighted by coloured lanterns, and the lords and ladies strolled about followed by musicians. Everyone could play a musical instrument and write verses with graceful strokes of the brush. The *Tale of Gengi*, written by Lady Murasaki in Japan at the beginning of the eleventh century, gives us a vivid picture of the life of a court which, although Japanese, must have resembled in many essentials that of Ming Huang. The volumes of this tale describe a state of culture vastly superior to that existing in Europe at the same time. We read of poets and painters and beautiful women, living and loving when and where they pleased. Elegant courtiers, such as Queen Elizabeth liked to have about her, tread their careless way in and out of the story. Dressed in rich silks, they ride to court to pay their respects to their sovereign, or they hurry in disguise through the night to a secret tryst. Above it all, and yet by far the most important figure, sits the Emperor on his throne, the supreme arbiter of human destiny.

Transfer the *Tale of Gengi* to China and we have a picture of the court of Ming Huang, painted as no prose artist has painted it before or since. Then let us imagine Yang Kuei-fei the centre of the scene, her tall form bending like a reed as she dances the 'posturing dance' before the Emperor, or sings to amuse him and his guests.

Yang Kuei-fei had three beautiful sisters, and with the generosity of one who fears no rival, she brought them all to court to share in her good fortune. Their names were Yang Han Kuo, Yang Kuo Kuo, and Yang Ch'in Kuo, and they seem to have accepted the Emperor's intimate favours indiscriminately. Yang Kuo Kuo was the most beautiful of the three sisters and the most independent. The Emperor gave her a fine horse to ride and a dwarf eunuch to care for it. All three sisters and their two brothers were given great houses in which to live, as well as many servants and much gold, and the extravagance of the five households of Yang provided the country with something to gossip about. An extract from the Chin T'ang Shu describes the Yang clan riding out:

'Husan Tsung (Ming Huang) on each progress to the Palace of Glorious Purity, was accompanied by Yang Kuo-chung, his elder sisters and younger sisters of the Five Households and their retinues. Each household consisted of one company wearing clothing of one colour. When the Five Households united their companies they glowed and shone like flowers. In their abandon they dropped hair ornaments and threw off shoes. Their jades, crystals, pearls, and kingfisher ornaments were resplendent, brilliant; as they passed sweet fragrance was wafted down the road.

'Furthermore, Yang Kuo-chung, who had secret relations with Yang Kuo Kuo, did not avoid sharp wounds from the strong fox of suspicion.

'Their saddle trappings pressed together, their chariots joined in a square, not using curtains or screens, the Five Households followed the Royal Progress to Hua'ch'ing, Palace of Glorious Purity.

'From this can be estimated in what manner the Festival to uproot Evil on Third Day Third Moon, must have been like.'

The Emperor, no doubt, found the society of these lively ladies amusing, for he often offended propriety by leaving his palace and dining with the five households of Yang. The 'Flowers of Yang,' as the ladies

were called, although married women, went in and
out of the palace as they pleased. Tu Fu, the poet,
hints darkly·

> '*Mystery surrounds revels at Palace heart.*
> *Few there were of outer people who knew.*'

Tu Fu must have been thinking of the safety of his
own head when he described the ladies of the court
in the following poem, probably written to please the
Emperor. The reference to their virtue is meant to
be ironical, as no one knew better than Tu Fu how
little of this particular quality they possessed.

'*Third Moon, third day, Heaven's breath new;*
Ch'ang-an water's edge, many dazzling ladies.

Of gracious demeanour, far-reaching ambition, and virtue
moreover undeviating;
Their skin fine of grain, glossy and smooth; bones and
flesh well-proportioned.

Upper garments, lower garments, of embroidered silk
gauze, reflect gleaming light in the sunset month of
spring;
It beats down on gold peacocks and silver Ch'i Lin.

Upon their heads what is there?
Ornamental leaves made of kingfisher feathers droop past
the line of their lips from hair bound on the temples.

Their backs behind, what can be seen?
Pearls pressing down loins, skirts hanging straight, their
*   bodies perfectly fitted.'*

As a subtle compliment to its beautiful mistress, the palace given to Kuei-fei by the Emperor was called P'eng Lai, after the abode of the Immortals in the Jade-Grey Sea. Seven hundred women were kept there to weave and embroider her clothing, including the garments of embroidered silk gauze referred to by Tu Fu in his poem. Flowers appropriate to the different seasons and symbols of her rank were embroidered on her robes by skilled fingers. Hundreds of other women lived in the palace and made gold and silver objects for her use. It is hardly surprising that this abode of a human immortal should have given rise to many legends. It was even whispered that little hornless dragons appeared in the pools, and occasionally found their way to the imperial canal, where they could be seen playing together.

Tu Fu tells us in one of his poems that the Emperor's stables contained 'forty-three ten thousand horses,' under the care of a noted horse breeder. Like his ancestor, the Emperor T'ang T'ai Tsung, Ming Huang was passionately fond of horses, but while the founder of the dynasty mourned over those slain under him in battle, and caused their portraits to be carved in stone and placed near his own tomb, Ming Huang had his taught to dance, a significant change in the point of view. Four hundred of the finest horses in his stables, called 'proud horses' because of their unusual height, were taught to do all manner of tricks in time to music. Covered with silk nets, and with jade and pearls braided in their flowing manes, they performed 'posturing dances,' holding cups filled with the 'wine of longevity' in their teeth. On the occasion of the Emperor's birthday, called the Feast of a Thousand Autumns, something very much like our modern circus seems to have taken place with the 'proud horses' playing a prominent part in the festivities to the delight of the court.

In the spring, when the peonies were in full bloom, and the peach and pear blossoms transformed the imperial gardens into a fairy world fit for Titania and her court, the Emperor would ride forth on a splendid horse called 'Shine White in the Night,' and Kuei-fei would accompany him, not on horseback like her sisters, but seated in all modesty in a wheeled palace chair.

The Emperor's tastes were many and varied. Five hundred soldiers were detailed from more violent forms of military exercise to care for his fighting-cocks. This was a sport beloved of Ming Huang, and as a young man he had often slipped out of the palace in disguise when a good fight was about to take place. Now that he could gratify all his tastes at home, thousands of these birds were kept for his amusement. The leader of this branch of his army was a young man whom the Emperor had once seen manipulating a mechanical cock. Ming Huang was so pleased with his skill that he loaded the youth with gold and fine clothes.

We do not know what the poets and artists who came to this brilliant court thought about the cocks and horses. Probably they were glad enough to share with them the lavish gifts of the Emperor. Tu Fu seems to have been a transient guest, because, owing to the corruption existing in high places, he never passed the necessary examinations during the reign of Ming Huang to become a permanent official of the state. During the following reign he was appointed a censor, but before that time he had been very poor and one of his children even died of starvation. His career was an unsatisfactory one from a financial point of view as his circumstances changed with great rapidity from the luxury and plenty which an association with the court provided, to the most extreme forms of poverty. Once, when he presented three appropriate poems to the Emperor, he records:

'Heaven's Son left his food and issued a command.
I joined the band of noblemen who use fine chariots and wear fine clothes.'

But this happy state of affairs never lasted for any length of time. Tu Fu was too honest and too sincere a patriot to keep in the good graces of the court officials forever, and more often than not he found himself a homeless wanderer, hard pressed to find the means of sustenance for himself and his family.

Li T'ai-po, China's greatest poet, was another
visitor who came to the court and sang of the charms
of Yang Kuei-fei when he was provided with sufficient wine to stimulate his muse. For a time he
enjoyed a life of luxury, but he was often intoxicated,
and his rude manners gave offence to the courtiers
although they only seemed to amuse Kuei-fei and the
Emperor. Once when the poet was drunk, Ming
Huang ordered the chief eunuch, Kao Li-shih, to
pull off his boots, thus unwittingly making a powerful
enemy for Li T'ai-po. It was the eunuch who later
secured the poet's banishment from court by in-
sinuating to Kuei-fei that the famous poem, in which
the poet compares her to the 'Flying Swallow,' a
notorious beauty of the Han age, was not intended
as a compliment but rather as a veiled insult to
herself.

> '*Pray who in the glorious Han Palaces,*
> *Can we compare to our own Emperor's lady,*
> *Save Flying Swallow clad in all the freshness*
> *Of her incomparable loveliness?*'

As a parting gift to the poet, Ming Huang commanded that he should be furnished with wine free
of charge in every wine-shop throughout the Empire.
An act of imperial bounty which possibly shortened
his life, as one warm summer's night, when on a
boating excursion with friends, he mistook the reflection of the moon in the river for a visitation of

the moon-goddess herself, and without hesitation he plunged into the water to join her.

Wu Tao-tzu, another visitor to the court, was not only the greatest painter of the T'ang age, but the greatest that China has ever produced. So sure was his brushwork that when he drew the aureole of a god with one single stroke of the brush it was said that a supernatural being guided his hand. Wu Tao-tzu was commissioned by the Emperor to decorate the walls of the Taoist temples which were then being erected. None of his frescoes have survived, but contemporary literature describes their beauty.

There is a hint of a Taoist mystery in the disappearance of the artist which occurred when he had finished a magnificent painting on one of the walls of the palace. The picture had been concealed by a curtain which the Emperor drew back in the presence of the court, revealing a marvellous landscape. 'Look,' said the painter to the Emperor. 'In the cave at the foot of this mountain dwells a spirit.' He clapped his hands and the door of the cave flew open. 'Allow me to show you the way.' So saying he passed within, the gate closed after him, and before the Emperor could speak the picture had faded from the wall leaving no trace. Wu Tao-tzu, the darling of his age, had likewise disappeared for ever.

Ming Huang was a patron of the drama, as well as of all other forms of art, and performances for both the court and the public were given in floating theatres on the lakes and canals. But music was even a greater joy and he had an orchestra of between five and six hundred pieces arranged in a square, conducted by one man as our orchestras are conducted today. The beauty, the art and the luxury of the whole world was at his disposal—and it was as nothing to him compared to the love of Yang Kuei-fei.

It would seem as if in this wonder city of Ch'ang-an the lady would have found her heart's desire, but on the contrary, she quarrelled bitterly with the Emperor. When this happened he would send her to her elder brother's house, while a hundred carts, weighed down with jewels and personal belongings, made their slow way after her. But such a solution gave little consolation to the Emperor. He would sit and brood, touching no food, while the swish of whips sounded through the palace as the eunuchs beat those who displeased him. The state of gloom would only be dispersed when someone more clever than the rest whispered the welcome suggestion that Kuei-fei be asked to return. Then what a change took place. Riders were sent post-haste to fetch her back, the gates were flung open, and Kuei-fei returned to bend her tall form before the Emperor and admit that she had been in the wrong. Business of state would be forgotten while:

'Towards the pavilion of porcelain walks the Emperor, shining with his jewels; and leaves his grave Mandarins to look at each other in silence.'

Once when she had been sent away, Ming Huang relented after a day or so of solitude and sent her a gift of food from the imperial kitchens. Kuei-fei wept and said:

'The Unworthy One has been intractable before the face of the Enlightened One. Her faults deserve ten thousand deaths. Her robes, her apparel and all besides, are bestowed by the Grace of the Enlightened One: she has nothing to keep or bequeath. Her hair and flesh alone are from father and mother. With the sharp scissors she severs a tress of hair to offer up in expiation.'

Needless to say her return was not delayed, and she was seen once more in the halls of the palace. The position of Kuei-fei became even more powerful at court when her cousin, Yang Kuo-chung, was made Minister of the Right on the death of the former prime minister. He was a man of little learning and less rectitude, and seems to have possessed no other qualifications for his exalted post than his relationship to the reigning favourite. The Prime Minister soon found that the simplest and easiest way to make affairs run smoothly was to repress unfavourable reports. This gave him time to indulge in his own passion for drinking and gambling, and the Emperor was spared such unpleasant news as defeats on the border, rising food prices, or disastrous floods. Under the new regime palace intrigues became even more complicated than before, and the passion of the Prime Minister for his cousin, Yang Kuo Kuo, the sister of Kuei-fei, caused a fresh scandal. Their houses were side by side with communicating doors, and when they rode to court, their horses prancing on the road, 'not one but feared that propriety was being outraged.' Small wonder that the households of Yang were not popular with the people, who later were to hold them responsible for all their sufferings.

The ladies of Yang were not burdened with a rigid code of morals, least of all Kuei-fei, but she is only once accused of betraying her imperial lover. Once, in this case, was enough to destroy an empire. Although the love between Kuei-fei and Ming Huang has been compared to that of the heavenly lovers— the Oxherd and the Weaving Maiden who were only allowed to meet once a year, and then crossed to each other over a bridge of magpies—it would seem to those of a less romantic disposition that the Emperor loved and Kuei-fei allowed herself to be adored. It may have been that as the Emperor grew older his attentions were not the beginning and end of life to her as they were at first. Perhaps she found that someone more exciting was needed to give spice to the luxury to which she had grown accustomed, someone younger and more virile. It was the propitious moment for the villain of the piece to stalk across the stage. The scene was set for his arrival.

If An Lu-shan had never lived, the story of Kuei-fei and the Emperor might have gone on and on, until as an old woman, her beauty gone, she took her place among the forgotten wives and concubines in the secluded parts of the palace, while new and more beautiful favourites courted the smiles of the sons of Ming Huang. It is to An Lu-shan, as well as to the Emperor and the poet Li T'ai-po, that she owes her fame and reputation, and it is to the first that she owes her greatest debt, that of her early death. Unlike the unfortunate Plum Blossom, her predecessor in the affections of Ming Huang, she never found it necessary to lament the passing of her youth in a poem sent to her former lover. On the contrary, Kuei-fei will remain for ever as Li T'ai-po saw her, leaning against the scented balustrade in the imperial gardens, glowing with eternal spring. She died because for one brief moment she loved An Lu-shan but her fate might have been much more dreadful had she lived to an unloved old age.

An Lu-shan, a native of Lukchak, was of Turkish descent. His mother was believed to be a witch, and at the time of his birth a halo was seen round the house where he was born and the beasts of the field cried aloud. This strange occurrence disturbed the authorities so much that they sent for the child to put him to death, but his mother, the witch, succeeded in hiding him. The child who came into the world under such extraordinary circumstances grew up to be a tall, heavily built, clever youth. He had an astonishing knowledge of local dialects which saved his life when once again the authorities decided upon his death—this time for sheep stealing. A true soldier of fortune, he next turned his talents to border warfare and made a name for himself by repressing the raids of the Tartars. This success proved to be his stepping-stone to court.

The guileless and kindly Ming Huang took an immediate fancy to the young man, and Kuei-fei treated him with great familiarity. She called him her adopted son, and made him salute her before the Emperor. When his uncouth manners outraged the court, Kuei-fei and the Emperor laughed and attributed them to his foreign blood and lack of knowledge of Chinese ways. So great was his favour in the eyes of the Son of Heaven that jealousy was aroused and there were many who disliked and distrusted him. The Prime Minister was bitterly jealous and said to the Emperor: 'Lu-shan is of a treacherous pattern.' This remark was repeated to An Lu-shan by one of his spies, and after that time the enmity between the two men was barely concealed when they were forced to meet at court. When An Lu-shan revolted and took the road to the capital with an army of one hundred and twenty thousand men, he announced his intention of killing Yang Kuo-chung. Everyone hated the Prime Minister for this reason and thought him the cause of the disaster, although the part played by Kuei-fei behind the scenes was generally known.

The Yang clan was divided among itself on the question of An Lu-shan. Tu Fu, the poet, who records most of the events of the reign of Ming

Huang, does not speak of the love of Kuei-fei for the Turk, because, as a commentator remarked:

> 'If Tu Fu had said that Yang Kuei-fei kept An Lu-shan in her private apartments not only would the words be such as should not be uttered by an official of the Empire, but there would have been no poem.'

Others, however, were not so considerate of the feelings of those in high places and referred to the criminal passion between the Turkish general and the lovely Kuei-fei. Some say that she was aware from the beginning that he intended to seize the throne of China for himself and reign in the place of the old Emperor with her as his queen.

There were others at the court besides the Prime Minister who wanted An Lu-shan out of the way, and eventually the Emperor himself became suspicious. The revolt of a northern tribe provided a welcome excuse for sending the young man away in spite of the complaints of Kuei-fei, who said she disliked being parted from her adopted son. He left the capital to return to the army in command of some of the best troops of the Empire.

During the next few years An Lu-shan, thanks to his many victories, rose step by step until he reached the rank of *wang*, or prince. Ming Huang, forgetting his former suspicions, was overjoyed at the success of his general. He accepted all his recommendations for promotion, and in this way An Lu-shan managed to permeate the army with officers and men of his own choosing. His arrogance and pride grew with his rank. He refused to obey regulations, and at one time showed his contempt for the Emperor by remaining in his tent when an imperial messenger arrived at the camp. All the country people were aware that he was collecting horses by tens of thousands and storing up grain and other foodstuffs necessary for war. Everyone except the Emperor expected him to revolt. But the Prime Minister, consistent to the end, continued to repress disturbing reports, and Ming Huang, in his blindness, thought that all was well.

An Lu-shan was eventually placed in command of all that part of the country which now includes Pei Ping and when finally he gave up the last pretence of loyalty and proclaimed himself Emperor, a serious crisis was expected. Bad news such as this could no longer be kept hidden, and at Ch'ang-an all was in confusion. The Emperor wished to appoint the Heir Apparent as regent and lead his troops himself against the enemy, but the Prime Minister was terrified and called the ladies of the Yang clan to his aid. He knew that if the Heir Apparent came into power they would all be killed. Kuei-fei herself went to the Emperor dressed as a suppliant, a clod of earth between her lips. Her grief touched his heart and he gave up the project in order to remain at her side.

The defence of the Empire was put into the hands

of the fiery old general Ko-shu Han, who had had long experience of revolts and border-warfare. Left to himself, he might have successfully accomplished the task entrusted to him, but the evil counsels of the Prime Minister interfered with his plans. The General wished to wait for the rebel army at the T'ung Kuan Pass, an almost impregnable position, but Yang Kuo-chung, dominated by his hatred of An Lu-shan, wanted the latter destroyed as quickly as possible. The Emperor was therefore induced to issue orders for an advance. Han, with a heavy heart, and against his better judgment, led his men through the pass to meet the invader, and suffered a crushing defeat. His army was annihilated, and the general himself taken prisoner. After that there was nothing to stop An Lu-shan from advancing on the capital.

The people living in the path of the oncoming army were terrified and fled with their families to a place of safety. Tu Fu, the poet, was among their number, and started off on foot with his wife and children. His description of the flight is told in the following poem:

'*My heart recalls our escape at the beginning of the rebellion;*
Fleeing northwards, we endured dangers, difficulties.

For an eternity my entire household stumbled forward on foot;
The People we met were all coarse and brazenfaced.

199

The land rose, uneven, irregular; birds called in the
*   ravines;*
We did not see a single traveller returning whence we had
*   come.*

For a period of ten days the roll of thunder alternated
*   with a downpour of rain;*
In mud, in mire, we dragged, clung to one another.

Since we lacked resist rain preparations,
Our garments were cold; the paths slippery as glass.

At times we suffered great hardship and bitterness,
Covering but a few li during an entire day.

Wild fruits constituted our provisions, our food for the
*   journey;*
Low branches provided the rafters of our dwelling.'

Terror seized the inhabitants of Ch'ang-an. A
chain of bonfires between the city and the army had
been lighted every night to inform the Emperor that
the pass was still held. One night there were no
fires, and flight was instantly decided upon. Just
before dawn Ming Huang left the palace and rode
away. With him went Kuei-fei and her sisters, her
cousin the Prime Minister, the Heir Apparent and
his family, a few court ladies and the chief eunuch
Kao Li-shih. The city was abandoned to the rebels.
Tu Fu says:

*'At this moment Imperial consorts, ladies of lesser rank are
    massacred;
How many will rot and become dust?'*

The unfortunate Emperor proceeded through a
downpour of rain. At daybreak he crossed the river
and when he had passed the bridges were destroyed
to prevent pursuit. No food was obtainable as the
post-houses were empty and the officials had fled.
When the Emperor stopped at noon to rest beneath
a tree, an old peasant women brought him a dish of
millet, which he ate with gratitude before he hurried
on his way.

By the second day the soldiers who were escorting
the party and who had been unable to obtain food,
were furious. Their rage demanded a victim and
the officer in command, who was afraid they would
revolt, addressed them as follows:

'Now all below the sky falls in ruins, is scattered; the ten thousand chariots of the Imperial
forces are shaken, are ready to overturn. Is this
not because Yang Kuo-chung has pared and peeled
the ignorant country people? Officials who serve
at court, men out of office, are bitterly resentful
(saying) "Has he brought us to this?"'

'If we do not kill him and thus gain the gratitude
of all below the sky, how can this deep resentment,
stretching to the Four Seas, be checked?'

All replied: "Indeed we have thought this for a

long time past! If in carrying out the matter our bodies die, we are willing they should do so.'' '

At these words all the hatred that had slumbered for years in the hearts of the populace against the five households of Yang burst into flames. The soldiers had but one idea—to kill. Hunger was forgotten as they fell on the Prime Minister and hacked his body to pieces. The sisters of Kuei-fei fled, but they were hunted like wild beasts, captured, and slain. Then the soldiers turned their attention to the shrinking woman, hiding behind the Emperor in the post-house. Crowding about the building, they demanded the life of Kuei-fei.

It is said that the Emperor hid his face in his sleeve when he heard the shouts of the soldiers for Kuei-fei. For nineteen years she had been his greatest joy and his life would be empty and meaningless without her. The chief eunuch pressed him to act. The soldiers would revolt, he said, and the dynasty would be lost. He begged the Emperor to think of the lives of his sons and grandsons. Kuei-fei, knowing that she was doomed and fearing a worse fate, threw herself at the feet of Ming Huang and confessed her part in the conspiracy of An Lu-shan, saying that she had sinned and merited death.

Even now the Emperor hesitated, but there was no time to be lost as the shouts of the soldiers were becoming more menacing and he had no choice. In a moment they would be in the post-house, dragging away the woman to whom he had devoted the best years of his life. Reluctantly he gave the order. The chief eunuch took her into an adjoining room, where he adjusted a silken cord about her neck and hanged her.

In a short space of time he returned. In his arms was the limp body of the dead woman, which he carried to the window for all to see. Shouts of 'Long live the Emperor!' greeted him as he stood there with his burden, but they brought no consolation to the old man huddled in one corner of the empty room. That was the moment when Ming Huang died, although the spirit lingered in his body for a number of years to come. With the passing of Kuei-fei passed also his importance as a ruler. No longer was he destined to be a prominent figure on the stage of the world. The 'Bright Emperor' was no more, and in his place was a tired and broken old man. Hastily the body of the concubine was wrapped in purple hangings stripped from the imperial coach and thrown into a hole by the side of the road. There was no time for a proper burial, and with one last look at the resting-place of his beloved, the Emperor slowly mounted his horse and continued on his way to exile.

An Lu-shan did not live long enough to enjoy the fruits of his victory, but soon met with an ignominious death at the hands of his own son in the palace at Ch'ang-an. The following laconic account is given in the T'ang histories:

'The son used a great knife, hewed his (Lu-shan's) belly; his bowels gushed out upon the bed; he died. The affair was notorious.'

That was the end of the rebellion as well as of An Lu-shan. The Heir Apparent, who had been left behind after the tragedy at the post-house, succeeded in raising a new army and was able to reconquer the capital. While Ming Huang remained in exile, his son was proclaimed Emperor under the name of Su Tsung. He too, had suffered, and when the ceremonies of his coronation were over the tears ran down his face. An upright man, although not possessed of a forceful character, he restored the dynasty to its former position of power, and peace returned once more to the land.

But the brilliance of the reign of Ming Huang was not to be recaptured by his successors. It had been a glamorous interlude when the arts had flourished as never before and when the splendour and luxury of the court had reached its highest point. For a time the sun had shone on Ming Huang and his lovely lady, and in the warmth of its rays genius had given birth to beauty as is only possible during a protracted period of peace. Such moments were rare in the history of the great Empire which he governed with such an airy touch, and if moon-fairies and facts mingle indiscriminately in the fantastic pattern of his life, it must not be forgotten that real children of the gods such as Li T'ai-po, Tu Fu, and many others lived at his court and sang his praise. His romantic history had a lasting influence on the arts and literature, not only of his own country, but of the neighbouring state of Korea, and it was a poet of the latter country who wrote the following poem in memory of an Emperor's love—the beautiful Yang Kuei-fei.

'Remembering the stories told of her,
I turn the ghost leaves of a shadow book.
Each touch of her light hands, each drowsy look
From her camellia petal-shaded eyes,
Were like the butterflies
That float from character to character
All down this ancient poet's painted scroll—
Which now on rods of ivory I roll,
And, wrapped in silken fragrance, lay aside.

So, silently remembering, I hide
Her name, inscribed in tablets of my soul.

Out of five thousand, not one character
Could tell her beauty nor my tears for her.'

Yu Hsuan-chi, the poetess-nun, and her servant

VIII

A TAOIST NUN:
YU HSUAN-CHI

[DIED 872 A.D.]

'Once upon a time I, Chuang Tzu, dreamt
I was a butterfly, fluttering hither and
thither, to all intents and purposes a
butterfly. Suddenly I awakened, and there
I lay, myself again. Now I do not know
whether I was then a man dreaming I was
a butterfly, or whether I am now a butterfly
dreaming I am a man.'

'CHUANG TZU.' TRANSLATED BY
H. A. GILES

Characters in the Story

YU HSUAN-CHI   *A poetess-nun of the T'ang dynasty*

LI TZU-AN   *The husband who abandoned her*

WEN FEI CH'ING   *Known as Wen, the Flying Minister*

VIII

A TAOIST NUN

IN the year A.D. 854, during the reign of the T'ang Emperor Wu Tsung, the Buddhist religion in China was subjected to a violent persecution. Four thousand six hundred temples were destroyed, while more than two hundred thousand monks and nuns were forced to return to secular life. Priceless treasures were lost to posterity, including many works of art created by the great masters of the T'ang dynasty and innumerable objects of Buddhist sculpture dating from an earlier period. For the moment China had renounced the alien religion of Buddhism, which had been brought with so much danger and difficulty by learned monks across the mountains from India, and the people substituted in its place an older religious system that had been indigenous to its own soil.

This religion was called Taoism and was based on the mystical teachings of Lao Tzu, the Sage who lived at the time of Confucius in the fifth century B.C. It was not the first time that Taoism had been supported by an Emperor and patronized by the court, but after this last Buddhist persecution Taoism had begun to incorporate within its rituals and beliefs so much of the doctrine of the Buddhists that some of the external differences between the two religions were lost. A Taoist monastery in the ninth century A.D. was a cluster of buildings, much as a Buddhist one had been, and Taoist monks and nuns in white or 'sad-coloured' garments worshipped their gods and studied their sacred books far from the haunts of men in the same way as the Buddhists had done for centuries.

The Taoist doctrine of 'The Way' was always difficult to understand and indefinite in its application to daily life. It lent itself to many and varied interpretations, and in the course of time the followers of the Sage forsook his cryptic utterances to dabble in the congenial art of magic. The name given to the gown worn by both monks and nuns was the 'Robe of Feathers,' symbolizing the claim of the Taoist magician to fly through the air, while the design on his shoes referred to his supposed ability to walk on the clouds. An important part of monastery life was the cultivation and preparation of herbs, as it was the ambition of the Taoist priesthood to distil from certain plants an elixir of life. More than one emperor had prematurely ascended the dragon—the polite form of announcing his death—in an effort to achieve immortality, and on more than one occasion a solicitous minister had begged his sovereign to beware of beverages brewed by the Taoists. At this period of their ascendancy we find a minister addressing the throne as follows:

'I humbly pray that all those who present to your Majesty their concoctions, may be compelled first of all to swallow the same periodically for the space of one year. Thus will truth be effectually separated from falsehood.'

Aside from preparing elixirs which so often proved to be exceedingly potent poisons, the monks and nuns spent their time attempting to 'sublimate' the Yin, or emotional side of their nature, and to substitute in its place the Yang, or higher self, so that they could 'achieve the supreme, positive self which returns to its source.' When not engaged in this ambiguous pastime they were free to do very much as they pleased, as their lives were regulated with none of the severity practised in the monasteries of the West. There were no vows of poverty, chastity, or obedience, and the individual novice could make visits or receive friends in his private apartments.

Even the cultivation of the arts was not discouraged. A gifted monk or nun could practise calligraphy, write poetry, or paint pictures, as such a one brought fame to the monastery where he lived. Many accusations were brought against them because of the freedom of their lives, and a later writer refers to a monastery as 'a term which is simply another name for a house of ill-fame.' The life of Yu Hsuan-chi amply demonstrates the fact that there was some truth behind this statement and it was openly said a hundred years before her time that the Emperor

Ming Huang visited Yang Kuei-fei at night during her period of purification in a Taoist nunnery. Doubtless there were good as well as bad monasteries, and Yu Hsuan-chi, like Yang Kuei-fei, was anything but a typical daughter of China. They were both wayward beauties who indulged their own whims and ignored the conventions and prejudices of the age in which they lived.

Yu Hsuan-chi is interesting as a type of woman which the later T'ang produced. It was an effete age, when many lesser poets wrote verses of a tender beauty unique in Chinese literature. They knew a great deal, too much perhaps to be original, and their work was filled with innuendoes and references to moods. Yu Hsuan-chi herself was a poetess of no mean ability, although her genius has been overshadowed in the eyes of posterity by the literary giants who lived and wrote only a short time before her. Such names as Tu Fu, Li T'ai-po, Po Chu-i and many others made the poetry of the T'ang dynasty famous for all times, and it is not to be wondered at that little is heard of the songs of Yu Hsuan-chi, who, like the Chinese painters of the Sung dynasty, expressed a mood rather than an event.

The poetry of Yu Hsuan-chi is the mirror of her life, which was influenced entirely by her emotional reaction to her environment. Endowed with a fine brain, it would appear as if she never used it to direct her own life, but, like a leaf, was blown hither and thither by the autumn wind. It was a harsh blast of this same wind which took her off the streets of Ch'ang-an and landed her in the draughty halls of the Taoist monastery of Boundless Contentment in the hills beyond the much lauded capital city. Her destiny was bound up with this monastery and yet few women have ever lived who have been less suited to spend so many years of their lives in an endeavour to 'sublimate the emotions' and follow 'the Way of the Tao.'

'Young and Tender' was the name by which Yu Hsuan-chi was known to her contemporaries in the streets of Ch'ang-an. Before she was sixteen years of age she was famous for the excellence of her calligraphy and for her ability as a writer of songs. Her biographer thinks that she was the daughter of some poor scholar, who had devoted a certain amount of attention to her education and had given her a basis of culture which made her seek the society of students and poets. These were kindred spirits who could appreciate her wit, and with whom she was able to hold her own in intellectual pursuits. She seems to have envied those fortunate males who had the advantages of a higher education, and she wished she had been a man so as to follow in their footsteps.

During these early days, free to come and go as she liked with the fascinating city of Ch'ang-an as her playground, it is doubtful if the eyes of Yu Hsuan-chi ever once turned towards the Monastery of Boundless Contentment, as boundless contentment of quite another kind reigned in her own heart. She had a lover. He was exactly the type of lover that such a girl would have chosen. Young, handsome, as irresponsible as herself, with all the opportunities which she lacked to cultivate his mind and eventually to graduate into the privileged class of officialdom, Li Tzu-an symbolized everything that the heart of the budding poetess could desire. He sent her presents and she replied with songs. Even at the beginning of their association it is apparent that Yu Hsuan-chi loved and that the brilliant young student, waiting for the day of his examinations, allowed himself to be adored. She speaks of being 'buried in this dull street,' eagerly waiting to meet him. And again she says:

> '*Before the red gate leaves sift through the air—*
> *Oh, sweep them not away, but leave them there,*
> *Waiting for One-who-knows-the-heart to come!*'

No doubt Li Tzu-an was flattered that the beauty of Ch'ang-an, courted by innumerable students, should be ready and willing to accept from him,—'The precious mat, new spread in Pied Kingfisher Hall'—a present which suggests the intimate relationship between the two lovers. He had a wife at home whose existence it was convenient to forget until after the examinations, and in the meanwhile what could be pleasanter than the carefree life of a student at the capital with a lovely mistress who appreciated the 'golden coloured wine' as much as he did himself.

Far from the Confucian standards of propriety were the love songs which flowed in an unending stream from the writing brush of the 'Young and Tender' blossom of Ch'ang-an, and one can easily imagine how such outpourings of affection added to the prestige of the young man in the eyes of his fellow students and made him a person of importance in his group.

This period of the life of Yu Hsuan-chi, while her lover was waiting to go up for his examinations, was the happiest that this talented but unhappy woman would ever know. A true Bohemian, she gave no thought to the morrow but took what each day had to offer. Her poems reflect her eagerness for beauty, for lofty pines and for the wistaria which grows on high mountains. Her sorrow is recorded when rain debarred them from visiting the 'Hat-falling heights,' the name for any hill sufficiently lofty to endanger the safety of the hat upon the head. These and similar joys and sorrows occupied her mind, and not until Li Tzu-an passed his examinations and graduated as an official into the rank of 'Hatpin and Tassel' did reality, long since relegated to the background, break through her dreams. Then faced by his impending departure, in an agony of fear she writes:

'Now suddenly, again the Immortal Youth will go;
Even in sleep, oh, do not say whither the cloud
*   will blow!*
One wild moth flies about the dimming light . . .'

But the 'wild moth' was to have one last moment of delirious fluttering before the 'dimming light' went out for ever. The Candidate Li decided to make her his concubine and take her back with him, along with his few belongings, to his ancestral home. Blissfully ignorant of what the future held in store, this child of the streets of Ch'ang-an set forth with her lord to face a future of provincial respectability.

The position of a secondary wife in the home depended to a great extent upon the good will of the first wife, and Yu Hsuan-chi was not the type of woman to be welcomed with open arms by the average matron. In this case the two women belonged to different worlds, and it was not long before the Candidate Li discovered that love songs and golden wine would not be tolerated in a respectable home. The Chinese character for home is a pig under a roof, and Li was to learn to his sorrow that the addition of a pair of mandarin ducks—the symbol of conjugal love to which the poetess so often compared herself and her lover—in no way added to the good temper of the pig. In fact, although Yu Hsuan-chi scrubbed floors and did house-work until she was pale and thin, no effort of hers could please his other wife, and the situation became so strained that Li found it more comfortable to remove the cause of contention from the home and hide her away in a mountain retreat. How much the girl from Ch'ang-an enjoyed the change is evident from the following poem:

A TAOIST NUN

'Arms full of books, the Silken One may stray,
  Or, indolent, float in the painted boat and croon
    to the Moon,
While softly winds blow to and fro.'

It was all beautiful at first, but gradually the harassed husband allowed the time between his visits to his love to lengthen, and as autumn brought in its train shorter days and longer nights the 'Silken One' began to realize that her situation was indeed desperate. She became homesick for the sound of 'washing paddles,' the autumn accompaniment of women's talk as they wash their husband's winter clothing in the stream, and she writes to her husband:

'Not of steep mountain trails or perilous ascents
  Will I complain, but of the hard, hard ways of love.'

On Li's occasional visits the two would get drunk together, and those were joyous occasions, but later, as Yu Hsuan-chi found boredom and gloom gathering about her and when she writes of being idle with nothing to do, 'abandoned in the wilds, with time to spare,' she began to drink alone, a habit which she never afterwards renounced. The poem that she wrote at this time called 'Voicing Deepest Thoughts' reflects the life she was then living.

'Then, the book finished, on the couch I drowsily recline,
  Rising half drunk to comb my hair.'

When the books had all been read and the wine-jars emptied, Yu Hsuan-chi realized that the husband she adored would come no more. There was no place for an abandoned wife in the social system of her day, and the girl from the city requested that she might be permitted to divorce the man who had deserted her. Such an attempt was unheard of, and this, like every other gesture made by Yu Hsuan-chi, was doomed to failure. When her request was refused she realized that only two paths lay before her. One led to the houses of pleasure where lived the courtesans of Ch'ang-an, and the other, the harder, steeper path, led to the Taoist Monastery of Boundless Contentment. Broken in health, her beauty impaired by tears and steady drinking, the frail figure of the poetess might have been seen making its way up the hill to the mountain retreat. One can imagine her shrinking back before the door was opened to admit her, hesitating for the last time before she entered the enclosure which must have seemed to her like a retreat for lost souls.

Among the many buildings which made up the Monastery of Boundless Contentment were temples and halls for public worship, guest-houses, libraries, as well as the living quarters for monks and nuns. Yu Hsuan-chi was welcomed with enthusiasm as her fame as a poetess had preceded her. Quarters were assigned to her where she could have privacy and access to her beloved books. Her solitude had made her crave company, and therefore her mood lightened when once more she found her talents appreciated by others less gifted than herself. Many great ladies became Taoist nuns during the latter part of the T'ang dynasty and Yu Hsuan-chi may have found pleasure in their society. In a nunnery as elsewhere, 'Among the truly educated there is no distinction of class.'

In the beginning of this phase of her career the poems of Yu Hsuan-chi reflect a certain measure of contentment. Although her heart was broken she could still enjoy the simple pleasures of monastic life. She writes of visiting her tutor or chanting in the choir of the Blue Damsels, as the nuns were called by the poets. She had her duties to perform, but they were light ones: steeping herbs on 'the warm clay stove,' or brewing tea in a nearby court. For recreation she had her dreams of the past, her reveries, which took up so much time that she confesses to leaving her Taoist books under her pillow unread while she wandered off to loiter on the hillside or sit beneath the willows by a brook. As time wore on she felt increasingly forsaken and alone, especially in the autumn, which was always a time of distress for her. She felt that age was creeping on her although she was still in her early twenties, and she searched for the white strands which she thought would soon begin to show in her dark hair. In the evenings she would stand on the terrace and watch the lamps as they were lighted one by one in the houses of the city. Poor Yu Hsuan-chi, born for love and happiness, to whom the humblest duty of a happy wife was an inspiration for a poem, what strange trick of fate had taken her to the aery where she stood?

If the Taoist nun gazed with longing eyes towards the city, there were those in the city who sent equally longing glances up the hill towards the monastery. It was not so many years since a 'Young and Tender' beauty had been the toast of Ch'ang-an, and there were those who remembered her verses and her wit. Pilgrims made their way from the city to the monastery on the hill, and among their number were brave gentlemen from Ch'ang-an hoping for a glimpse of the pretty nun. To the bored and despondent woman their coming was a boon. Happy once more she received them in her apartment, or feasted with them on the hillside. Again the wine flowed and the party would break up with the dawn. Oblivion was to be found in the wine-jar if not in the Taoist ritual, and anxious lovers soon found that the nun was willing to be comforted in a manner which suited them quite as well as it did her.

Among these lovers was a battered disreputable poet by the name of Wen Fei ch'ing, or Wen, the Flying Minister, as he was called. A native of the province of Shansi, he had made his way to Ch'ang-an in order to sit for his examinations and eventually graduate into the class of officials. Wine, women, and other forms of dissipation had proved his undoing, and instead of acquiring the rank of Hatpin and Tassel it is recorded in the T'ang Annals that:

'One night when drunk Wen Fei ch'ing quarrelled with a disreputable companion, one I Ho,
who in a fracas pummelled the poet and knocked
out several of his teeth.'

Episodes such as this did not add to his good
standing in the eyes of the local authorities, and finding that his services were not required by the
Emperor, Wen moved to the outskirts of the city,
where he lived surrounded by the rogues of his day,
in total disregard of even the most elementary of
conventions.

It was quite in keeping with the reputation enjoyed
by this eccentric man that he should become en-
amoured of a Taoist nun, and between his visits to the
monastery on the hill we find him writing verses to Yu
Hsuan-chi: 'In your feathered chaplet you are like a
chick on a coral tree,' he writes, referring to her symbolic head-dress of feathers. And at the same time he
jestingly accuses her of stealthily hiding away the yak-
tail whisk, a Taoist emblem of spirituality, to steal to
the arms of a lover by the willow bank. A little later,
when his heart had been completely captivated, he
writes of her as one who is full of charm, a real
moon fairy who has become the inspiration of his
muse.

This poetic flattery must have sounded very sweet
to Yu Hsuan-chi and she responded with details of
her own hard lot:

'*Under the lamplight reading verse with unassuaged
regrets,
Not sleeping through the whole long night, dreading cold
coverlets.*'

There was no passion in the poems she sent to the
Flying Minister. She never loved him as she had loved
the husband who deserted her, but she was heartily
tired of the monotony and hardships of a monastic
life, and Wen wooed her in a manner which she
found irresistible. He held out to her the prospects
of travel. Friendship she had for him and a deep
affection, and the end was inevitable. The 'chick on
the coral tree' abandoned her feathered head-dress
and returned to the world as the mistress of the
poet, who, in the fullness of his love, now compared
her to a jade-tree in the Phoenix Hall.

It may have been that the need of money first
turned the footsteps of the literary lovers towards the
ancestral home of the poet in Shansi, but wiser than
the former husband of the lady, Wen did not attempt
to take her all the way with him. He left her at a
sufficient distance from his home so that no news of
his travelling companion should reach the ears of his
parents, and went the remainder of the way alone,
leaving Yu Hsuan-chi to amuse herself as best she
could during his absence. If he wrote poems while on
the visit to his parents they have not survived, but
Yu Hsuan-chi has sketched a portrait of herself as she
was during the period of waiting:

'*The wayfarer grows drunk on the red counterpane;*
Inkstone and writing brushes near,
Walled round with books and verses here.'

That visitors knocked at her door is recorded in other poems, and basking in the admiration of provincial officials the time passed pleasantly.

It may be presumed that Wen's journey home proved to be successful and that he returned with funds, as we next find the lovers embarking on an ambitious project. This was no less than a voyage up the Yangtze, that mighty river which flows from the mountains of Tibet to the sea. It was an unheard of journey for a woman to make in a land where women never travelled for pleasure and the vagabond poetess, wandering from city to city, and from temple to monastery, seeing all there was to be seen of interest, must have created a scandal. But scandal or no scandal. it was a glorious experience for Yu Hsuan-chi. Her knowledge of history had prepared her for the trip on the river, and the poems which record the journey are filled with historical and classical allusions. Both poet and poetess responded to the sights they saw.

Soon after they embarked they saw in the distance the mountains of Chu Lo, famous as the birthplace of Hsi Shih, the beauty of a thousand years before their time. Here was an inspiration for a poem not to be missed and Wen writes:

'*Beside the Hall of Hsi Shih by Yen-ch'eng's city wall*
The willow branches stretch their hands in mute appeal to all.

Their shadows on the river with those of sails compete;
Their nearer bendings brush the bank with salutation
    sweet.
What bound the Wanderer's heart-strings and bade him
    turn again
Was not the verdure of the grass all lush with vernal
    green.'

The poem suggests that Wen, the Wanderer of the poem, was comparing himself to Fan Li, the faithful lover of Hsi Shih, and that in the eyes of both men, separated from each other by a thousand years of time, the charms of a fair travelling companion were more important than the most entrancing of spring landscapes.

Such a compliment must have sounded pleasant in the ears of the former nun, and she responded with a poem of her own about Hsi Shih. This, as well as many other bits of historical landscape, inspired both travellers and their brushes flew over the paper as they recorded their individual reactions to some incident of the past. One virtue the Flying Minister certainly possessed: he did not attempt to change the woman who had joined her life to his, but accepted her as she was. She did not have to pretend with Wen. Lying in the boat, 'drinking, drowsing, waking, sighing in a daze,' she was free to abandon herself to mystical reveries and speculate on the meaning of Taoism, dreaming like Chuang Tzu, the Taoist philosopher, that she was a butterfly. Or she would give way to moods of gloom, when rain washed the walls of the inn where they were staying and the strangers were regarded with suspicion. Gay or sad, religious or drunk, Yu Hsuan-chi was very much herself on this journey, sharing the pleasures and hardships in equal measure with the man at her side.

How long they were gone and why they separated on their return to Ch'ang-an is not known. The departure of one man and his replacement by another was not of sufficient importance to be mentioned in the verses of Yu Hsuan-chi. True to her first love, her husband, the other men in her life, including Wen, were only incidents. Even during the journey on the river she had written poems in the form of letters to the man who had deserted her so long ago. Perhaps Wen left her because he was tired of possessing a woman with a broken heart, who meant more to him than he would ever mean to her. It would appear from the following poem as if he left her at Ch'ang-an and returned to the river alone:

'*Alone upon this river tower*
What gloomy thoughts my heart devour!
Like waters still the moonbeams flow.
The river joins the sky below.
But where are they who with me came
To gaze upon her lambent flame?
The scene is much like last year's: yet
Those gone how can my heart forget?'

That was the end of Wen as far as Yu Hsuan-chi was concerned, but she found much at Ch'ang-an to console her for his departure. She established herself in a fashionable part of the city and celebrities flocked to her door to visit the woman who was not only known as a beauty and a poetess, but who could now entertain them with strange tales of far-off lands and adventures which doubtless lost nothing through retelling. It was a gay time for Yu Hsuan-chi and many poems record her successes with the lovers who came to her house.

But being once again without a protector, there were many pitfalls for the vague footsteps of the former nun in a man-made world. She forgot the old saying of the Chinese people that ill-regulated virtue ends in reputation, and ill-regulated reputation ends in notoriety. Too good-natured and too easy-going to turn away the disreputable acquaintances of former days, who came to her in ever increasing numbers, she slipped lower and lower down the social scale. Her more reputable friends ceased to visit her, poverty knocked at her door, and with her usual frankness she writes of pawning her embroidered dresses and her dusty mirror and toilet set.

It was at this period of her career that she wrote her most celebrated poem, called 'Selling Wilted Peonies,' which her biographer uses as the title of her book on the life of Yu Hsuan-chi. In this poem the poetess looked at herself in the mirror, as it were, and examined the failure which she had made of her

own life. Why, she wondered, when endowed with
so many gifts, had the world passed her by? But still
optimistic, she cries:

> *'Yet set this shoot in the imperial court,*
> *And lords will covet what they may not buy.'*

Poor Yu Hsuan-chi, for her there was to be no
imperial court. Her footsteps were leading her to
quite a different court: the court of law, and the
sordid squalor of prison as the prelude to an ignominious death. Her life was drawing to a close, but
she was unaware of the fact. Bewildered and im-
practical to the end, she did not see the writing on
the wall.

It was about this time that she first came into con-
flict with the police. For a long time the authorities
had looked with suspicion on her friends and her
manner of life. Now, for some reason or other, she
refused to pay the tribute demanded of her by a minor
police constable for protection, and in this way made
for herself a dangerous enemy. Perhaps she would
have paid had she had the money, but there was wine
to be bought with the proceeds realized by the sale
of embroidered dresses, and the dusty toilet set and
mirror suggest the habits of a drunkard, who had
ceased to care about the externals of life. Careless of
the consequences, Yu Hsuan-chi sent the man away,
a mistake for which she was to pay dearly.

Finally, when all resources had failed her and all

her lovers had deserted her, she turned her eyes for the second time towards the Monastery of Boundless Contentment. There was no other refuge left for her. The years of wandering and adventure were over, the cycle was completed, and leaving hope behind, Yu Hsuan-chi once more entered the monastery as a Taoist nun. Sadly she resumed her head-dress of feathers and picked up the yak-tail whisk. Like the toilet set she had left behind her in the city, they were dusty from lack of use.

The story of the life of any other woman but Yu Hsuan-chi would have ended at this point. The monastery had welcomed her back. More than that, the authorities had given her a maid to wait upon her so that she would be spared the performance of even those light duties which had previously fallen to her lot. Her talents were appreciated, and within the confines of the cloister she should have found peace. But there was no peace in this world for Yu Hsuan-chi. One day news was brought to the city that the poetess-nun had murdered her maid.

The story that was circulated was long and complicated. The body had been found by the same minor constable who had previously been unsuccessful in his attempt to extract money from the impoverished woman while she was living in Ch'ang-an. Suspicion pointed to the nun and it was said that she was jealous of the younger woman who could now attract the lovers who had once sought the society of the poetess herself. Yu Hsuan-chi was taken to prison and tried for her life. At first she did not appear to be unduly disturbed about her position. In a poem addressed to a neighbouring girl, but really written about herself, she still clings to the idea that a lover will come and save her. 'Hard, hard to win a lover kind and true!' she laments, while 'tears wet the pillow of loneliness.'

Sentence could only be passed in a medieval Chinese court on one who had confessed, and some biographers of Yu Hsuan-chi believe that she had nothing to confess. Tradition asserts that she was guilty, but it seems probable that the maid was killed by the constable who had found the body and who had then accused the mistress of the crime. If she was innocent there was only one way that a confession could be wrung from her—torture. It was a legitimate method and many different kinds of torture were used. We do not know whether it was the finger-press or the application of the boot which in the end broke the frail spirit of Yu Hsuan-chi, but the necessary confession must have been extracted from her as she was sentenced to be decapitated by the sword.

In the year A.D. 872 the verses of this gifted and uphappy woman ceased for ever. Her head, severed from her body, rolled in the dust of the prison courtyard, and her body was flung on to the refuse heap outside the city walls.

IX

PRECIOUS PEARL:
EMPRESS OF THE MING DYNASTY
[DIED 1644 A.D.]

'Only the gentle breezes of the spring
Caress her little pair of lovely shoes.
Where are you now, O sad and fragrant flower?
It is too late to make a song for you.
Not all the singing of a hundred years
Could bear away the loneliness you knew
In one uncounted hour of falling tears!'

FROM 'THE ORCHID DOOR.'
RENDERED FROM THE KOREAN
INTO ENGLISH BY JOAN S.
GRIGSBY

Characters in the Story

PRECIOUS PEARL

The wife of Hsi Tsung, Emperor of the Ming dynasty

THE EMPEROR HSI TSUNG

Her husband

THE EARL OF EXALTED STRENGTH

Her father

MADAME K'O

Foster-mother of the Emperor

WEI CHUNG-HSIEN

Chief Eunuch and Prime Minister

THE EMPEROR CH'UNG CHEN

Brother and successor of Hsi Tsung

LI TZU-CHENG

The rebel general who destroyed the Ming dynasty

IX

PRECIOUS PEARL

THE famous red pill had done its deadly work. The Emperor Kuang Tsung, Son of Heaven for the short space of two months, lay dying, and his heir, a weak, puny boy of fifteen, stood by his bedside to receive his father's last blessing. The dying man looked about him in despair. Where was there an honest man in whose care he could leave his son? He looked into the evil face of his father's infamous chief eunuch, the notorious Wei Chung-hsien, and he heard his concubines quarrelling as to who would be Dowager-Empress after his death. The others were no better. Why had he, with short-sighted kindness, pardoned their many plots against the dynasty and allowed them to retain their positions at court? The Emperor realized that this time his enemies had triumphed and that he had failed—failed because he had neglected to clean out the Augean stable left to him by his own father.

He was dying and he knew it; dying from slow arsenic poisoning administered by the eunuchs after a direct attempt at assassination had been unsuccessful. He may not have known that it was poison which was sapping his strength, but he felt that his hours were numbered. Better get it all over quickly and have done with it. He was tired of fighting against the web of intrigue spun by women and eunuchs, the double curse of decaying dynasties. So he asked for a second red pill, as dubious of origin as the first, and assigning his soul to the care of Heaven, he 'ascended the Dragon' in the year 1620 when he was thirty-nine years of age.

When an emperor dies there is no telling how many of his subjects may be affected by his death. Millions may suffer because of the passing of a man whom they had never seen, and in those difficult times when the power of the Ming dynasty was in its decline, and strong, virtuous rulers were only a memory, thoughtful men were troubled because they knew not what evil would result from the death of their king. There was no hint as yet that the country was on the brink of one of those dreadful periods of cataclysm, when civil war and foreign invasion would take their toll of the strong as well as the weak, but people were apprehensive and disturbed. The new Emperor, Hsi Tsung, was an undersized boy of fifteen. What chance would he have against the corruption that haunted the palace and oppressed the people as they worked on the land?

Thoughts such as these must have passed through the mind of a wise and kindly scholar who lived in the province of Honan. He was worried. A dissolute brother of the late Emperor had recently taken up his residence not far away, and the eunuchs who

supplied his harem with women had cast covetous
eyes on the scholar's own daughter, the beautiful and
virtuous Precious Pearl. To be sure, she had in-
dignantly repulsed them, and even threatened to take
her own life if force were used to remove her from
her father's house, but the good scholar was much
perturbed. Who would protect his family now the
Emperor was dead?

Precious Pearl was a daughter by adoption, not by
birth, but the scholar loved her as if she had been
his own child. One winter's day, many years before,
he had found her, a tiny girl-child, lying half-frozen
by the roadside. He had taken her home, warmed and
fed her and brought her back to life. As she grew into
a beautiful and diligent young woman he himself had
taught her to write the difficult Chinese characters
with fine sure strokes of the brush. Many other things
he had taught her as well, but best of all, in the eyes
of Precious Pearl, he had taught her to love the Lord
Buddha, and to take her troubles to him as the source
of all ultimate wisdom and love. Yes, his Precious
Pearl was an exceptional woman. He would have
liked to marry her to his eldest son and have her
always with him in his home, but he hesitated to do
so. A learned Bonze who had read her horoscope
prophesied a great future for the girl, and who was
he to interfere with the workings of Karma?

Precious Pearl herself must, as a devout Buddhist,
have believed in Karma, that is to say, that the events
in the life of the individual were predestined before

birth. She knew, of course, that she owed her life to her adopted father, whom she loved with tenderness and devotion. Later he was to be given the title of the Earl of Exalted Strength. Perhaps she chose that name for him herself as she knew that his noble character entitled him to such a designation. But she did not know—how could she?—that two red pills administered to a dying Emperor were to change her whole life.

When the young Emperor, Hsi Tsung, reached the age of sixteen, eunuchs were sent throughout the length and breadth of the land to choose the most beautiful maidens between the ages of thirteen and sixteen, to compete for the honour of becoming his wife. The good scholar of Honan must have remembered the prophecy of the Bonze when, after a preliminary look at Precious Pearl, the eunuchs returned the next day for a more detailed inspection of her charms. Thousands of young girls were carefully examined, but when the choice had narrowed down to three hundred, Precious Pearl was still included in the number, and with the others went to take up her residence in the palace for a month's probationary period. During the month all those who were disobedient or showed signs of stubbornness were eliminated until only fifty remained, all of whom were appointed imperial concubines.

There yet remained the all important position of Empress to be filled by one of the fifty already chosen to be concubines, and for this great honour a certain amount of education was necessary. Those who could not use the writing brush to advantage were not considered eligible. Precious Pearl and two others were finally selected for their culture as well as for their beauty, and these three were brought before the Emperor for him to make his choice.

The senior concubine of his grandfather, who had assumed the authority of an Empress-Dowager, had examined the candidates in the more subtle refinements of their education. She had been much impressed with Precious Pearl, as she thought her a lovely and accomplished girl. This lady was present when the Emperor made his choice and spoke in favour of the girl, although the Emperor's foster-mother, the notorious Madame K'o, used her influence to make him decide upon another candidate. Madame K'o, who was a beautiful but evil woman, took an instinctive dislike to Precious Pearl; a dislike which was to have lasting and far-reaching results. Her influence with the Emperor was great, but this time she could not persuade him to renounce one who had already charmed him. Following the dictates of his own heart, as well as the advice of the senior concubine, he selected Precious Pearl to be his Empress. The two other young ladies were given the titles of the Virtuous Concubine and the Pure Concubine.

When Precious Pearl became Empress the forces of evil were already united against her. The infamous chief eunuch, Wei Chung-hsien, who had been in-

strumental in conniving at the death of the late
Emperor, but who yet stood high in the good graces
of his son, had made an alliance with Madame K'o,
and little by little the government of the state was
slipping into their grasp. The young Emperor had no
idea of the duties and responsibilities of his position.
He enjoyed using his hands instead of his brain and
devoted his time to carpentry and other similar
pursuits, which brought him into contact with those
of a lower station in life than himself. When busily
engaged with saw and chisel he disliked being disturbed, and when Wei Chung-hsien came to him for
instructions he would send him away and tell him to
do as he pleased. Soon all official documents were
written for the Emperor by the eunuch and read:
'We and our Eunuch Minister decree as follows——'
The people were seriously alarmed when they saw
how this dangerous man was allowed to assume control of the government, and brave censors sent
memorials of protest to the throne, but with no result. The memorials were suppressed and honest
officials were removed from their posts.

The only way to reach the ear of the Emperor was
through Wei Chung-hsien or Madame K'o, and even
princes of the blood and viceroys were forced to pay
tribute to the powerful minister. He demanded
honours for himself second only to those accorded
to an emperor, and when he went abroad he was
greeted as the Lord of Nine Thousand Years; the
designation of Lord of Ten Thousand Years being

reserved for the Emperor alone. Millions groaned under the crushing taxes he imposed, while at the same time his own wealth increased and gold and silver poured into his private coffers. The terrified people built shrines to propitiate him and worshipped him as a god, and they even went so far as to compare his wisdom to that of Confucius. Wise and good men who were not in favour of his policy were cast into prison and in many cases were tortured to death so brutally that, when their bodies were returned to their relatives, they were quite unrecognizable.

Unnecessary brutality has always played a part in Chinese history whenever the eunuchs have assumed control of the state. It would seem as if these creatures wished to be revenged on a society which condoned their mutilation. They appeared to lack the most elementary sentiments of either gratitude or compassion, and there are countless incidents to prove that the sufferings of others gave them pleasure. Once in power, the eunuch was the most brutal of masters, who delighted in the use of poison and torture. The evil deeds of Wei Chung-hsien and others like him destroyed the prestige of the Ming dynasty and 'it fell as other dynasties did before it, because of the inherent want of moral qualities, without which no power will ever be long tolerated by a people like the Chinese, who demand so high an ideal in the Sovereign.'

The fall of many of the great Chinese dynasties has been preceded by the rise to power of the eunuchs.

It was their policy to corrupt the boys of the imperial house, devoting especial attention to the demoralization of the future emperor. A youth trained by the eunuchs from an early age to indulge in every form of vice could be easily influenced once he ascended the throne. In many cases weak emperors also fell under the domination of their consorts, whom, however, the eunuchs found less easy to control. By reason of the democratic marriage customs of the Chinese, imperial brides were chosen from the ranks of the people and they had the inestimable advantage of passing their youth away from the enervating influences of the Forbidden City. It was the salvation of Precious Pearl, as well as of many other empresses, to have spent their youth in touch with reality; whereas their husbands often perished at an early age from the results of habits of dissipation acquired during a childhood spent within the walls of the palace.

The eunuch Wei and Madame K'o were sufficiently astute to recognize a natural enemy in Precious Pearl, whose fine, incorruptible character would be opposed to any form of vice. While they were unable to prevent her elevation to the position of Empress, they resolved to do everything in their power to make her life at the court unendurable. The slights and humiliations which were inflicted upon her are recorded in many memorials sent to the throne by the censors, who deeply resented the position in which the Empress found herself. She was treated with indignity, and while she waited for her own simple meals the eunuch and Madame K'o were provided with all the delicacies that the empire could provide. Spies surrounded her who reported her every move, and even stories were invented regarding her birth and paternity in an effort to discredit her with both the Emperor and his subjects. It was said at one time that she was the daughter of a murderer on trial for his life.

To all these attacks Precious Pearl paid not the slightest attention. She passed her days in reading and embroidery or taught penmanship to those of the concubines who were intelligent enough to desire to learn. Many hours were spent in prayer before her shrine, where an image of the Lord Buddha looked down upon her with holy calm. When life at court became especially difficult she would dress herself in the robes of a nun and spend her days in fasting and meditation.

> 'Slender and white as jade were her lovely hands;
> Dark as the soft wings of night was her hair;
> Tender as golden bells was her voice—
> Strained towards far distant hills were her eyes.'

The distant hills, towards which the true mystic looks with unseeing eyes, were always the source from which Precious Pearl drew her strength: strength that was like that of the reed which bends but is never broken, which bows before the wind, but stands upright when once again the storm is over.

It must be said, however, that the young Emperor was devoted to his beautiful wife, although he neglected to give her the honours due to her rank, and failed to protect her from the attacks of her enemies. The gentle counsels of Precious Pearl were the only influences for good that ever touched his life, but they were frustrated by the more powerful suggestions made by his foster-mother. Many attempts were made to remove Madame K'o from the palace as her presence there was contrary to custom, but when she yielded to the clamour of public opinion and retired to her own residence, the health of the Emperor suffered, and she was always speedily recalled.

Precious Pearl must have been a woman of extra-ordinary intelligence as well as of unusual beauty, for she was never the dupe of her enemies and was always aware of their ability to do her harm. She knew all about the methods that were being used to undermine the health of the Emperor and place him in a position of impotence, and whenever it was possible she did what she could to save him from his fate. When he was given drugs to stimulate his passions, Precious Pearl would take possession of the drugs and throw them down the well. Sometimes the Emperor would break away from his evil companions and dine with his wife or take her rowing on the lake. On such occasions her beauty and goodness would charm him, and she would find the opportunity to advise him to improve his mind and study the classics. But such moments were rare, and they were quickly forgotten by the Emperor once he returned to his customary habits.

During the lonely years of her married life the Empress suffered one of the greatest misfortunes which can afflict any woman. Her child was born dead. When she first entered the palace she was allowed to have about her women of her own choosing, but these ladies-in-waiting were soon removed and either killed or imprisoned by the eunuch and Madame K'o. Their places were taken by women in the pay of her enemies and they spied upon their mistress and reported her words and actions. When her child was expected one of these women, a masseuse, so mistreated the Empress that the child did not survive. The miserable Emperor was unable to protect his own offspring; a fact which was pointed out to him in a memorial addressed to the throne.

At one time the Emperor was almost induced to abandon his wife when a woman of great beauty was introduced into his harem and given the status of a Jen concubine. When her influence was at its height an attack was made against the father of the Empress, who had previously received the title of earl. All his honours were taken from him, but when Precious Pearl heard that her adopted father's life had been spared, she dressed herself as a supplicant and thanked the Emperor on her knees for his mercy.

Once, and once only, did the Empress attempt to break the power of her enemies by attacking it at its source. Surrounding herself with an armed guard, she called Madame K'o to an audience in the Palace of Feminine Tranquillity. There, seated on her dais, the Empress told the woman to prepare to die for her sins. Madame K'o fell on her knees and begged for mercy, and while the precious moments slipped by a eunuch had time to run and warn the Emperor of what was taking place. Hurriedly leaving his carpentry he arrived in time to save the life of his foster-mother.

At the age of twenty-three the Emperor fell ill with what proved to be a fatal illness. During his last days Precious Pearl moved in and out his chamber, bringing solace to him through her gentleness and love. She nursed him tenderly as long as there was any hope of his recovery, but when she saw that his days were numbered she took action and begged her husband to nominate his brother as his heir. The dying man objected as he said he had been told by Madame K'o that two of his concubines were with child, but Precious Pearl spoke to him long and earnestly, and the result of her words was that his brother, Prince Hsin, was called to his bedside and nominated Heir Apparent. The prince wished to protest on the grounds that he was unworthy of such an honour, but the Empress once more assumed control of the situation and ordered him to obey his brother's request. After Prince Hsin had been appointed successor to the throne, the Empress led him to an inner apartment of the palace, where she kept him hidden, for she feared he might be assassinated by the partisans of the chief eunuch, who would be certain to attempt to establish a regency.

When the Emperor passed away, Precious Pearl fainted from grief and exhaustion, but upon regaining consciousness her first thoughts were for her brother-in-law and the necessity of preserving the dynasty. She insisted on his being immediately escorted to the Main Hall of Audience to receive the obeisance of his ministers. The eunuch Wei and Madame K'o dared not openly disobey these orders, but the Empress knew the character of her enemies and she feared that an attempt would be made to poison the new Emperor. She warned her brother-in-law to eat nothing prepared in the palace, and she sent her own confidential maid to market to procure food for him, which she cooked with her own hands. During the first days of the new reign Precious Pearl watched over the Emperor, and it was largely due to her efforts that he survived the intrigues directed against him.

The Emperor Ch'ung-chen showed his gratitude to his sister-in-law, who was now Empress-Dowager, by recalling her father to Peking and restoring to him his former honours. He held his brother's widow in high esteem, and during his reign she was regarded with love and veneration not only by the Emperor and his family but throughout the country. The people called her by the affectionate title of the

Goddess Chang. For many years she devoted her life to good works and lived a peaceful existence in her own quarters in the Forbidden City.

The first task of the Emperor Ch'ung-chen was to destroy his two greatest enemies. Madame K'o was put to death by the slow slicing process and all her family was executed with her. Wei, the eunuch, knowing that his end was near, escaped from the palace, only to be hunted down by the soldiers. When at last he found himself cornered he committed sucide. His head was exhibited in his native town and all the people rejoiced at the death of their oppressor.

The Emperor Ch'ung-chen proved himself to be an able ruler, but no one man could cope with the disintegrating forces that were undermining the dynasty. If he had dealt as drastically with all the eunuchs as he had with Wei, he might have survived and his family with him, but unfortunately only half-measures were taken and other eunuchs were left in positions of importance and were even given command of the army and of the defence of the palace. When the revolt, headed by the rebel general Li Tzu-cheng, broke out, there was no one who could check his advance. Money raised by taxes to increase the size of the army had been spent for other purposes, or had gone into the pockets of unworthy persons, and those in command had only one idea: to better their own situation in life. Surrounded by traitors and cowards, there was no way by which the

Emperor could repair the damage which had been done by generations of misrule.

The rebel Li Tzu-cheng was a fine general, and in a short space of time he made himself master of several provinces. The people were indifferent as they had lost their confidence in the Ming dynasty, and in many cases the eunuch commanders surrendered to the enemy in order to save their own lives. Inside the Forbidden City everything was in confusion. During the last days before the city fell, those who had been entrusted with its defence spent their time in feasting or in hiding their money in preparation for escape. On the day when the rebel troops were battering down the gates of the city one of the chief eunuchs gave a theatrical performance, after which many of his guests went out to meet the enemy and welcomed him to the city. The following words, written on a wall of the palace, showed the state of mind of the court:

'If this dynasty's star has waned, let us hitch our fortunes on to its successors.'

The wretched Emperor was left to his fate. He attempted to send his sons to safety, but it was already too late, and after the capture of the city they fell into the hands of the rebels. For himself, his wife, and his daughters there was no choice but suicide. The Empress hanged herself, and when the Emperor saw her dead body he killed one of his daughters with his own hands and ordered the others to follow the example of their mother. His last act was to write a message to his people on the lapel of his robe. It was found after his death.

'My virtue is small, and therefore I have incurred the anger of Heaven, and so the rebels have captured my city. Let them disfigure my corpse, but do not let them kill one of my people.'

Before he died the Emperor sent word to his sister-in-law, the Empress-Dowager, advising her to commit suicide. In the confusion Precious Pearl never received the message, but when she realized that the day of the dynasty was over, she attempted to hang herself. She was prevented from doing so by her attendants, who refused to allow her to take her own life. At this moment her courtyard was entered by the soldiers of the rebel chief, who had been ordered to find the imperial concubines and bring them to their master. The soldiers were astonished by the beauty and dignity of the woman they saw before them, but they were ignorant of her identity until the eunuchs of her household revealed her name and station.

One of the officers of the rebel army, who came from the same province as the Empress, determined to save her from the fate reserved for the concubines. He knew that such a woman would die rather than allow herself to be given to a man other than her own husband, and he thought to help her by interceding with his chief on her behalf. Leaving her in the care

of her attendants, he hurried away on his mission.
But before he returned the Empress had succeeded
in committing suicide. Her body was found dressed
in black silk with gold embroidery on the sleeves.
Her hair was neatly dressed, and her face covered
with yellow gauze. When the gauze was removed the
soldiers thought they saw before them a young and
beautiful woman. The face of the Empress was as
serene and peaceful as if she had at last entered into
the enjoyment of that happiness which had been
denied to her on earth.

Only a few faithful retainers witnessed the hurried
burial of the Empress-Dowager in the courtyard of
the palace where she died. For a long time afterwards the news of her death was not announced to
the populace, and as no one knew her fate, the Jen
concubine, who had been introduced into the palace
by Madame K'o, thought to enhance her own importance by pretending to be the former Empress.
The Jen concubine became the mistress of the rebel
chief and travelled about with him until the Manchu
armies from the north, aided and abetted by the loyal
Chinese general, Wu San Kuei, destroyed his army
as well as his hopes of founding a dynasty of his own.
After the Manchu conquest, the Jen concubine
established herself in the mountains north of Peking,
where her home became the meeting-place of lawless
men who forced the people of the surrounding
country to pay them tribute.

Enemies of the Ming dynasty had been only too

willing to spread the report that the Empress-Dowager had become the concubine of the rebel chief, and for many years her name was tarnished in the eyes of the nation by the woman who pretended that she had shared the throne with the Emperor Hsi Tsung. Eventually action was taken against the Jen concubine. She was brought to the capital to answer for her many crimes, and once there the impersonation was exposed. It is said that she was ordered to try on one of the shoes of the real Empress, a test which proved that her claim was false because the tiny shoe of Precious Pearl failed to fit her foot. However, on account of her former position in the Emperor's harem she was allowed to hang herself instead of being publicly decapitated.

After the arrest and death of the Jen the true story was made known and the name of the Empress cleared from any suspicion of slander. A eunuch, who had witnessed her death, came forward and told his story, and the body of the Empress was given a proper burial. The Ming dynasty perished in an orgy of bloodshed, and none regretting its passing, for its day was over. But the name of the woman who was affectionately known to the nation as the Goddess Chang remained unsullied. Although living in the midst of corruption, she had striven to combat the evil forces which surrounded her, and the example of this beautiful and virtuous empress will always be remembered by her countrymen in times of national distress and trouble.

The Princess Hsiang Fei

X

THE PERFUMED PRINCESS:
HSIANG FEI

'If the birds of the air are faithful,
How much more a pure woman.
Though she might have a virtuous mate,
Yet until life's end she must walk alone.'

'TYPICAL WOMEN OF CHINA,'
BY A. C. STAFFORD

Characters in the Story

THE EMPEROR CH'IEN LUNG	*Manchu ruler of China for sixty years from 1736*
HSIANG FEI	*Known as the 'Perfumed One.' A Princess from Eastern Turkestan*
THE SULTAN OF BADAKSHAN	*The ruler who decapitated the husband of Hsiang Fei*
A CHINESE GENERAL	

X

THE PERFUMED PRINCESS

FOR many centuries travellers from China, on their way to India and the West, were forced to pass through that inhospitable land which is now known as Eastern Turkestan. The dangers of the journey were immense. Waterless deserts as well as high mountains had to be crossed, while there was always the possibility of attack from some fierce desert tribe. It was a land to be dreaded by the traveller, but from the days of the Roman Empire, and perhaps long before, caravans laden with the products of China braved the dangers and hardships of the desert route.

Because of its strategic position, Eastern Turkestan has always been of immense importance to the Emperors of China. Strong rulers, from the time of the Han dynasty, sent military expeditions to conquer it, and maintained garrisons in different parts of the country to protect travellers. But at other times, when troubles at home occupied the attention of a harassed ruler, this outpost of the Empire would slip into foreign control, only to be reconquered with much bloodshed at a more propitious moment. Western races, some even of Aryan descent, filtered into Eastern Turkestan during moments of Chinese impotence, and in this way it became the home of many different peoples, who either because of religious persecution or economic necessity had been forced to leave their own countries.

In the course of time great cities, and even small independent kingdoms, occupied the oases in the desert. During the days of the T'ang dynasty a high civilization flourished in this distant part of the world, and Buddhist temples, Mohammedan mosques, and the churches of Nestorian Christians stood side by side, mute evidence of the diversity of creed as well as of race of those who occupied the land. Travellers from China, India, or Persia lingered in the cities to enjoy the comforts of civilization after their long battle with the elemental forces of nature, and they carried away with them tales of beautiful women, and strange stories of the luxurious courts of these isolated kings. Such tales lost nothing by retelling, and in the eyes of the world Eastern Turkestan became a place associated with romance as well as with danger, while the mystery which always surrounds remote places added an element of the supernatural to a culture which assumed legendary proportions.

But the fertility of the oases depended on one element, and one element alone—water. An elaborate system of irrigation had turned portions of the desert into gardens, but when the wars of Genghis Khan in the thirteenth century depopulated the country there were not enough men left behind to irrigate the soil.

Little by little the sands encroached until the cities, with their temples, palaces, and priceless objects of art, were partially blotted out. Sea routes took the place of land routes, and Eastern Turkestan, no longer the only highway leading from China to the West, deteriorated until it became the mere shadow of what it had been in the past.

During the eighteenth century, when Ch'ien Lung, the great Manchu emperor, sat upon the throne of China, the glory of Eastern Turkestan had faded, but it yet remained of sufficient importance for the Emperor to intervene when the two brothers who ruled the country, and who were known as the Big and the Little Hojas, started fighting each other. Ch'ien Sung sent an army to restore peace, and the brothers, who had no chance against the superior forces of the Chinese, were forced to fly for protection to the Sultan of Badakshan, the ruler of a neighbouring state.

One of the brothers, the Little Hojas, had a wife who accompanied him on his flight. She was known as the Princess Hsiang Fei, and her beauty was so remarkable that the report of her charms had spread throughout the length and breadth of her own land. Little is known about her early youth and married life except that she lived at Aksu with her husband, a city reached after six months of travel from Peking. But even though he was thousands of miles away, the Emperor Ch'ien Lung had heard of her beauty and of the mysterious fragrance which her body exhaled. So

255

wonderful was this fragrance that it intoxicated the senses of the men and women who approached her. It was whispered that her loveliness was that of a being from another world.

Like all men who saw the Princess from Aksu, the Sultan, with whom her husband had taken refuge, desired to possess her, and he thought to achieve his aim by having her husband beheaded and sending the head as a peace-offering to the Emperor at Peking. In this way he hoped to propitiate the Emperor and at the same time have the lady for himself. But the Sultan's schemes were circumvented by a contingency which he had overlooked and which proved to be too powerful for him. The Chinese general, sent by Ch'ien Lung to subdue the country, had received orders before his departure to bring the Princess back to court with him. Soon after the treacherous assassination of her husband, of which the lady was kept in ignorance, the Sultan received a demand for her surrender. There was no choice for him but to obey and he was forced to dispatch the following reply:

'Hsiang Fei is the most lovely of all Mohammedan women. To win her is not easy. To give up that perfumed flower is still harder. I will exchange her for ten pairs of rings of white jade from Honan.'

Perhaps the Sultan's decision was aided by the fact that his suit appeared to have little chance of success. Hsiang Fei, the 'perfumed flower,' was sunk in despair and neither threats nor persuasion could make her eat or drink. Both the Sultan and the general who received her in his tent after the ransom had been paid, feared she would take her own life as they were unable to arouse her from her lethargy. The general resorted to subterfuge and assured her that her husband was alive and on his way to Peking to be pardoned by the Emperor. He invited her to travel with the army until such time as she rejoined him at court. Her ladies were bribed to calm her, and all was made ready for the long journey to the capital.

The Chinese people have always been noted for their minute attention to detail, and the arrangements made for the comfort of the Princess on the journey were thoughtfully carried out. The wishes of the Emperor were law. The lady, like any other rare and precious object which he desired, must be delivered intact, that is to say, with her beauty unimpaired by the fatigues of travel. A six months' journey over desert roads would be an ordeal for any woman, so a carriage was prepared large enough for her to lie down in. The wheels were wrapped in felt so that it would ride easier, and curtains of brocade were hung at the windows. Two favourite ladies accompanied her on the journey, while twenty slave girls ministered to her wants and a guard of soldiers surrounded the carriage day and night.

The Princess had been accustomed to a daily bath of sheep's milk and kounis before her ladies rubbed her with the perfumes which had made her famous, and these unusual luxuries were provided for the journey. The friendly bleating of ewes with their lambs must have been heard as the army wound its slow way through the desert. Many romantic figures, including the famous traveller Marco Polo, have followed the same route before and since the days of Hsiang Fei, but no figure could be more romantic than that of the beautiful princess, reclining in her carriage while the gentle providers of the milk for her bath ambled behind with their young.

On the journey she would often talk and laugh with a youth who was believed to be the natural son of the Emperor Ch'ien Lung. When in the company of this boy, or alone with her ladies, she appeared to forget her sorrows and would laugh and play like a child. For the moment she felt herself to be safe. No man looked upon her with desire and no danger threatened her virtue. Although not a Chinese woman, Hsiang Fei had the Confucian point of view on the subject of marriage. She was fiercely loyal to her husband, who, dead or alive, was her master. As long as she lived she felt she belonged to him, and like many other women she preferred death to what she considered to be dishonour. The Sultan of Badakshan had realized that she would never allow any man but her husband to possess her body, and the Emperor Ch'ien Lung was to learn the same truth to his sorrow.

At the end of the long journey the victorious army,

with its beautiful prisoner, the princess from Aksu, reached Jehol, the summer capital of the early rulers of the Manchu dynasty. The palace at Jehol had been built by the grandfather of Ch'ien Lung, the Emperor Kang Hsi, the second and greatest ruler of the dynasty. Kang Hsi, like his ancestors and others of his race, was a great hunter. In the mountains surrounding Jehol there was game in abundance and every opportunity for the Emperor to enjoy his favourite sport. But Kang Hsi was a statesmen as well as a lover of sport, and he had a second reason for establishing himself during the summer months at Jehol. He wished to keep in touch with the Mongol princes, and as Jehol was outside the great wall of China and within the hereditary lands of the Mongols, it was a convenient meeting-place for them. Once a year they could gather there and renew their oath of obedience to their emperor.

Ch'ien Lung, like his grandfather the Emperor Kang Hsi, loved Jehol, and during his reign he built additional palaces and made more parks and gardens until his summer capital became a labyrinth of palaces, temples, pavilions, parks, and lakes. The Emperor knew and loved every corner of his vast domain, as he writes in one of his own poems:

'*I have visited every building on the hills and have explored the pine-decked valleys,*
Water, stones, mountain mists and flowers make a fairy land,

*Truly it is like a dwelling in the moon, far from the earth.
I delight in the joy of reading at the table by my study
window.'*

This was not an isolated poem written by the
Emperor. He wrote many others. Like so many outstanding Chinese statesmen, he was a great scholar
and his library at Jehol was world famous, while his
collection of art treasures exceeded in size and beauty
anything that had ever been known before. A wise
and kindly man as well as a fine ruler, the Emperor
Ch'ien Lung was worshipped as a god by millions of
his subjects and his fame had extended to the farthest
corner of the civilized world.

Such was the man who summoned the Princess
from Aksu to an audience after her arrival at the
palace. He was not one to be feared, and the Princess
did not fear him. Proud as the Emperor himself, she
stood before him silently weeping. The magnificence
which surrounded him did not impress her. The
greater he was the more difficult it would be for her
to escape from his power. Her reaction was one of
utter despair. Ch'ien Lung had been conscious of her
wonderful fragrance before she entered the apartment, but when he raised his head and looked at her
he was astonished. He thought that no one so
beautiful had ever been seen on earth before. For a
long time he sat watching her before he sent her
away with a gift of pearls.

It may have been that the blood of different races

mingled in the veins of Hsiang Fei and a blend of East and West might account for her extraordinary beauty. Father Castiglione, one of the Jesuit missionaries at the court of Ch'ien Lung, has painted her portrait, and very lovely she looks. But the costume the wise Jesuit chose for his model was a symbolic one. He painted her in full armour with a steel helmet and breastplate; the outward manifestation of that inward armour which she always wore in the presence of Ch'ien Lung. To Hsiang Fei, the Emperor was the murderer of her husband, and no kindness or consideration on his part ever caused her to think differently. Presents of luxuries or jewels had no effect. She did not even notice them, and when the Emperor visited her she would either remain silent or run away and hide at the top of the highest tower in the park, while her attendants made excuses for her and said that she could not be found.

When the Emperor was not present she could forget her sorrows and amuse herself with her ladies. One day as he approached her apartment he heard the sound of laughter, and he hid himself behind a curtain to watch unobserved. The Princess was sitting with her bosom bare, and her long hair flowing behind her. Lying on the floor at her feet were two palace girls, their breasts serving her as footstools, while the remainder of her women scrambled about the room after the pearls which she threw to them from a bowl in her hands. Although the pearls had been given her by the Emperor himself, he was much amused and entered the room laughing. The serving-women were terrified and fell on their faces before him. Hsiang Fei, on the contrary, appeared to notice nothing unusual. Slowly pulling out a mirror she started to dress her hair, showing by no look or indication that she was aware of the Emperor's presence.

Such treatment would have angered another man, but Ch'ien Lung was an exceptional person and he was convinced that kindness would win for him the woman he so much desired. He was too wise to take her by force. He waited, and while he waited his mind was occupied with ways and means of pleasing her. Acting on the advice of Ho Shen, his prime minister, the Emperor ordered a little Mohammedan town to be built for her when the court returned to Peking. The town was situated outside the south wall of the Lake Palace, and was constructed so as to resemble as closely as possible her own native town of Aksu, with bazaars, gardens, and a mosque where she could worship.

The idea of building a bazaar for the Princess must have appealed to the Emperor because he enjoyed bazaars himself. At the New Year he was fond of having a market fair in the gardens of his Summer Palace near Peking, and it is reported that he also had one for the ladies within the grounds of the palace of Jehol. All sorts of shops were set up, where curios, porcelains, and embroideries were sold. Restaurants and tea houses were freely patronized, and hawkers were allowed to come and sell their wares. At the New Year, as the Emperor passed down the line of booths, the waiters would shout out the menus for the day, hawkers would cry their wares and everything was bustle and noise, to the delight of the Emperor, who enjoyed all forms of gaiety.

Hsiang Fei could be gay too, but she would not be gay in the presence of the Emperor. When he took her to see the new town which had been built for her, she looked about her and wept. Her tears were a bitter sorrow to the Emperor, but he gave no indication of his disappointment. Later, however, she would often come and sit in the tower near the mosque where a holy mullah recited prayers to Allah the prophet; prayers which continued long after her death and only ceased in 1908 when the voice calling the Faithful was no longer to be heard from the mosque of Hsiang Fei.

The Princess was made a concubine of the fourth class, a Kuei-jen, which gave her a position at court, but which did not please her at all. A palace was especially built for her with a lovely garden where she could live undisturbed, waited upon by her Mohammedan servants. But one palace or another, it was all the same to Hsiang Fei. She was like a wild bird in a cage, and she pined for her dead husband and her desert home. So often did she threaten to take her own life that her attendants were ordered to guard her closely. It was feared at court that not only would she take her own life, but that she would attempt to kill the Emperor as well. Once when he entered her apartments after having drunk too much wine, he touched her on the arm. Quick as a flash she drew out her dagger, and would have stabbed him if he had not quickly moved aside. The point of the dagger, however, had touched his arm, which bled profusely, and before he could leave for his own palace her ladies were forced to bind up his wound, while Hsiang Fei wept and begged to be sent home.

After repeated requests from the Emperor, the Princess consented to dance the sword dance of her own country for him. The dance commenced slowly at first, but the pace quickened as she grasped the swords. Faster and faster she went while the swords flashed about her until, when it seemed as if she could go no faster, she rushed through the door leading into the garden and with one blow felled a pear-tree to the ground. In a minute it was all over. She was back in her place before the Emperor, motionless, cool and quiet, not one hair of her lovely head disarranged.

I do not know whether or not it has ever been suggested that Hsiang Fei was a fox-woman, but there must have been those at court during her time who believed that they saw before them one of that strange tribe which plays such an important part in Chinese myths and legends. According to this theory foxes could assume human form for a certain length of time, and they usually appeared in the guise of a beautiful woman. They bewitched men as Hsiang Fei bewitched the Emperor, and like her they were ungrateful and little appreciated kindness. A fox-woman, according to Chinese tradition, would have behaved as Hsiang Fei behaved to the Emperor, neither better nor worse, but one day she would have disappeared and would not have remained to die by her own hand as did the princess from Aksu. And yet it is reported that after her death this beautiful woman looked just the same. She seemed to be alive. The colour remained in her cheeks and her face was as lovely as before. So perhaps she was a fox-woman after all.

Even the Emperor may have thought her to be a fox-woman, for with all his wisdom he was not above believing in the superstitions of his age. In his youth a thoughtless prank on his part caused the death of a beloved court lady. Her name was Ma Chia, and the Emperor never forgot her, nor the wrong which he felt he had done to her. Many years later he believed he recognized the reincarnated spirit of Ma Chia in the person of a youth who had been chosen to be one of his litter-bearers. He called the young man aside and talked to him and in the end took him under his own protection and loved him as a son.

This man was Ho Shen, who later became prime minister and enjoyed power second only to that of the Emperor himself. He was given the daughter of his patron in marriage, and henceforth nothing was too good for Ho Shen. The Emperor loved him all his life, but Ho Shen betrayed the trust of his imperial patron, and it was due to him that corruption

crept in to undermine the wise and liberal government of Ch'ien Lung. Ho Shen planted the seeds that
led to the revolts which broke out during succeeding
reigns, and which at length caused the downfall of
the Manchu dynasty. Ch'ien Lung, like many other
men who have enjoyed great power, was unfortunate
in his loves. The woman he loved attempted to take
his life, and the man whom he trusted above all others
was instrumental in the destruction of his dynasty.

The infatuation of Ch'ien Lung for the beautiful
Hsiang Fei increased as time went on. Her ladies and
the eunuchs who surrounded her urged her to accede
to the Emperor's desires. She answered that if the
Emperor forced her to become his concubine in fact,
as well as in name, she would kill him as well as
herself. This was considered as a direct threat against
the life of the Emperor, and it was reported to the
Empress, who was already alarmed. Ch'ien Lung
could think of nothing but the wonderful Mohammedan woman. He would sit for hours in her apartments watching her silently even though she never
once glanced in his direction. He forgot to visit his
mother, and his health suffered from an infatuation
which left him no peace of mind and which caused
him to neglect his family and the state.

At length the Empress thought that the time had
come for her to take action, and having little influence
with her husband herself, she approached her
mother-in-law, the Empress-Dowager, and the two
ladies consulted together as to the best means of

removing one who appeared to them to be a danger to the dynasty. They made their plans together and prepared to act.

The time for the winter solstice was drawing near when, according to custom, the Emperor must spend three days in the Palace of Continence before he offered up the great sacrifice to Heaven. This was the opportunity for which his mother had been waiting, and as soon as he had left the palace she summoned Hsiang Fei to her presence. When the Princess stood before her the old Empress was astonished at her unearthly beauty. 'A fascinating devil!' said the Empress-Dowager. 'No wonder she has bewitched my son.'

She began to question Hsiang Fei. Was she grateful for all the kindness shown to her by the Emperor? The Princess replied that she hated the Emperor. She had been happy with her husband and the soldiers had taken away their land and killed the man she loved. The Emperor had pursued her with protestations of affection. She would have killed him long ago but he was too well guarded. Proud and erect, the Turkish girl stood before the mother and wife of the greatest ruler in the world stating her grievance. In spite of herself the Empress-Dowager was impressed. She asked Hsiang Fei in a kind voice what she desired.

At first the Princess asked to be sent back to her own land, and when that was refused she begged to be allowed to take her own life. 'I pray your

Majesty,' said Hsiang Fei, 'to give me the favour of death without my body being mutilated. Let me leave this world with my chastity unstained.' Throwing herself on the ground she repeated her prayer over and over again.

Perhaps the old Empress secretly sympathized with one who preferred death to remarriage. Certainly it was a point of view with which no Chinese woman could disagree. The most virtuous women, according to Chinese tradition, were widows who never re-married and who remained faithful to the memory of their husbands until death. So the chief eunuch was commanded to take her away and allow her to have her wish gratified. Before she was led to a room near the Moon-Flower gate to die by her own hand, Hsiang Fei bowed low to the Empress-Dowager. It was the first time she had shown either respect or gratitude to anyone at the court of the Manchu monarch.

Ch'ieng Lung was at the Hall of Fasting when a confidential eunuch brought word to him that Hsiang Fei had been summoned to the palace of the Empress-Dowager. Breaking the rule which required him to remain yet another day in seclusion, he hurried to his mother. With fear in his heart he asked respect-fully for the Princess. It must have been hard for the old Empress to tell her beloved son what had hap-pened, but with the serene conviction that she had acted for his good and for the good of the dynasty, she told him of the death of the beautiful woman he loved. She took his hand and urged him to repair the havoc that had been done to his health as well as to his heart.

Etiquette forbade the Emperor to utter a word of protest, and so he bowed his head. A eunuch took him to the room where Hsiang Fei lay in a coffin made for her by her Mohammedans. Never had she looked so lovely. The colour remained in her cheeks, and her body was scarcely cold. The Emperor wept as he looked at her. He closed her eyes and took a ring from her finger before he hurried away to face the reality of a lonely life without her. There were many other beautiful women in the palace, but no other ever took the place of Hsiang Fei in the heart of the Emperor Ch'ien Lung.

By his orders her body was placed in a simple tomb outside the great mausoleum, where eventually the Emperor himself was to lie. It was as near to his own resting-place as tradition would allow. No doubt he would have wished to have her buried with him, but this could not be. In death as in life he was separated from his beloved by an impenetrable wall.

Tz'u Hsi,
The Last Great Empress of China

XI

THE LAST GREAT RULER OF CHINA: TZ'U HSI

[1835–1908]

'Wealth, vice, corruption,—barbarism at last.
And history, with all her volumes vast,
Hath but one page.'

H. A. GILES, 'GEMS OF
CHINESE LITERATURE'

Characters in the Story

TZ'U HSI	*Empress-Dowager of China*
THE EMPEROR HSIEN FENG	*Her husband*
THE EMPEROR T'UNG-CHIH	*Her son*
A-LU-TE	*His wife*
THE EMPEROR KUANG HSU	*The successor of T'ung-chih*
THE YOUNG EMPRESS	*His wife*
THE PEARL CONCUBINE	*His concubine*
TA-AH-KO	*Appointed Heir Apparent to succeed Kuang Hsu*
TZ'U AN	*Co-regent with Tz'u Hsi*
PRINCE KUNG	*Brother of Hsien Feng*
PRINCE TUAN	*Leader of the Boxer movement*
JUNG LU	*Trusted adviser to Tz'u Hsi*
AN-TE-HAI	*Chief eunuch*
LI LIEN-YING	*His successor as chief eunuch*

X I

THE LAST GREAT RULER OF CHINA

IT is a strange coincidence that during the last half of the nineteenth century the two greatest rulers of the modern world should have been women: Victoria, Queen of England and Empress of India, and Tz'u Hsi, Empress-Dowager of China. Both women ruled over vast empires for many years, both lived to an old age, and both loved power, keeping the reins of government in their own hands until death loosened their grip. They both lived until the beginning of the twentieth century, but neither belonged to it; both in their own way were symbols of an order which they fought to maintain and which came to an end with their death. The small, dominating, intensely feminine personality of Queen Victoria is known to everyone in the Western Hemisphere, but comparatively few are aware of her Eastern counterpart, who possessed many of the attributes of the English queen.

The latter half of the nineteenth century witnessed a trial of strength between East and West, with China as the battle-ground, and the West won for the time being, although perhaps Tz'u Hsi never realized that disturbing fact. To the end of her life she modelled her policy on the ancient classics of her country, and when asked what she would do if China were defeated by a foreign foe, she quoted the words expressed by Chia Yi of the Han dynasty as a sound method of treating the conqueror: 'To simulate affection; to express honeyed sentiments; and to treat one's inferiors as equals.' The last point of the three is the important one to remember.

It was so much a part of the mentality of the Chinese people at the end of the nineteenth century to think of the foreigner as a barbarian and therefore one to be treated with contempt, that it is not surprising that Tz'u Hsi died as she had lived, unconscious of the fact that the changes which had taken place would cause anything more than a temporary inconvenience. Her policy was to sweep the 'foreign devils' into the sea, and when she failed to do so, the reforms which she was forced to make were instituted only to appease and throw dust in the eyes of these same inferiors, to keep them quiet, as it were, until a propitious moment should arrive for resuming the good old ways. The history of China since time immemorial has been one of conquest, assimilation— and in the end elimination, and who knows but that the future may prove Tz'u Hsi to have been right. Our 'brave new world,' with all the trappings of its material civilization, may yet be rejected by the East and crushed beneath the weight of an ancient tradition. When the Asiatic peoples have learned all that we can teach them they may succeed where Tz'u Hsi failed, and really push the 'foreign devils' back into the sea.

Fortunately for the peace of mind of the world of 1825, the coming struggle between East and West was still hidden in the womb of the future, although there were indications that trouble was on the way. The Manchu dynasty was in its decline. A succession of weak monarchs had destroyed the power and prestige of the earlier rulers of the dynasty, and internal revolts and external pressure made it seem probable that its days were numbered. Into this world, pregnant with unrest, a girl-child was born, with no sign from heaven to show that she was destined to hold back the inexorable march of time for half a century and to give her dynasty one last breathing space before it disintegrated for ever.

The birth of a girl-child has never been an occasion for rejoicing in China. Petitions were often addressed to the spirit world requesting the birth of sons to carry on the ceremonies of ancestor worship and the traditions of the race, but girls came into the world as a necessary but undesirable part of the scheme of things. The birth of Yehonala, the Orchid, afterwards known as the Empress-Dowager Tz'u Hsi, was no exception to this rule. There was no rejoicing at her arrival. The family was poor, and after the death of the father, the widow and children were cared for by a kinsman. This relative was the father of the girl who later became Empress-Consort of the

Emperor Hsien Feng. After his death she ruled the Empire as co-regent with Yehonala under the name of Tz'u An.

Very little is known about the girlhood of Yehonala. It has been said that she was betrothed as a child to her kinsman Jung Lu, a young officer of the guards, but whatever the circumstances of their early life and intimacy, it did not stand in the way of her entering the palace as concubine to the Emperor Hsien Feng. She was one among twenty-eight beautiful Manchu maidens chosen for this honour, and was given the rank of a Kuei Jen, or 'honourable person,' while the daughter of her kinsman ranked above her by becoming a P'in concubine and eventually Empress.

In practice an imperial concubine was little more than the servant of her mother-in-law, but Yehonala, because of her beauty and charm, soon established herself in the good graces of the Emperor and became his favourite wife. In 1856 she consolidated her position at court by giving birth to an heir to the throne, much to the joy of the Emperor, who until that time had been childless. It was not easy for a concubine of the third class to rise to the position of favourite, and Yehonala must have been an exceptional woman to do so. Portraits painted of her towards the end of her long life show her still beautiful, with a strong, intelligent face. It is unfortunate that no likeness exists of her during her young womanhood, when she must have been very lovely to look upon.

There were other qualities to recommend her when she entered the palace. She had had a good education according to Chinese standards. Every edict sent forth during her long reign contained some reference to the classics and she was never at a loss for an historical precedent to justify any action that she thought to be necessary, but, being a true woman, she ignored her knowledge of the past when she wished to break a law of her dynasty. She broke many laws, but never by mistake, and she usually excused herself by a clever quotation taken from one of the dynastic histories. Like many Chinese ladies, she painted with skill, and she could write verses, a necessary part of the equipment of court life.

Another fact which emerges from the study of her life is that even as a girl she had the ability to inspire others with loyalty and devotion. The story of her relationship with her kinsman Jung Lu is the best example of the faithfulness of those who served her, but there were many others. The rise to power of the two famous eunuchs, An-te-hai and Li Lien-ying can be traced to early days when, as her devoted slaves, they worked for her interests behind the scenes. As for Jung Lu, her former playmate, and possibly her betrothed, there is no doubt but that he became the trusted adviser to the throne, and served Yehonala to the day of his death. There is much to be said in favour of the woman who could turn the lover of her girlhood into her most faithful and loyal subject.

The husband of Yehonala, the young and dissolute

Emperor Hsien Feng, played an unimportant part in the history of his country as he, like many of his predecessors, lived a life of debauchery which ended in an early death. He was not, however, allowed to enjoy his vices in peace as his short reign was troubled by a succession of clashes between his troops and those of foreign Powers. Ever since the beginning of the eighteenth century attempts had been made by the Powers of the West, led by England and France, to establish facilities for trade, and to acquire places of residence for their merchants and officials in the cities on the coast. Such attempts had invariably been unsuccessful as, although the ambassadors from the West had been received with great politeness and had been loaded with gifts by Ch'ien Lung and other powerful Manchu emperors, no concessions had been made and their requests had been refused. From the Chinese point of view it had been a most satisfactory method of dealing with inconvenient demands and no doubt the same process would have been adopted by Hsien Feng had he been sufficiently strong to dispose of the Western Powers with a sweep of the imperial hand. Unfortunately for him, the West had discovered that when dealing with the Son of Heaven the sword was more effective than the pen, and in 1861 the position was reversed. A foreign army had gained control of the situation and was marching rapidly on Peking, while the Son of Heaven was preparing to retreat with his favourite concubine Yehonala and his young son to Jehol in Manchuria.

The health of the Emperor had never been good, and it became worse as the clouds upon the political horizon darkened. Yehonala, although only twenty-six years of age, was the mother of the heir to the throne, and as such had the right to an opinion. According to the diary of a doctor of the Han Lin Academy called *A Record of Grief Incurable*, she had a good deal to say on the subject of the court leaving Peking. 'The Yi concubine' (Yehonala), says the learned doctor, 'begged His Majesty to remain in his palace as his presence there could not fail to awe the barbarians and thus exercise a protecting influence for the good of the city and the people.' It was sound advice, but it was not followed and the court fled to Jehol. Prince Kung, the brother of the Emperor, was left behind to negotiate with the British and French. A treaty was finally arranged, but too late to save the Summer Palace, which perished in the flames with all its priceless art treasures and world-famous library.

The fact that Yehonala had the strength of character to oppose the wishes of important people and that she had urged the Emperor to remain in Peking, made her many enemies. It did not take unusual foresight on their part to perceive that, should she be appointed Regent after the death of the Emperor, she would be anything but a docile tool in the hands of those who wished to assume the power themselves. In Jehol, where her friends were few and her enemies many, she found herself surrounded by a group of hostile nobles who were sufficiently powerful to influence the Emperor against her during the last days of his life. It was only her resourcefulness and her ability to keep her head which saw her safely through a situation fraught with danger to herself.

This situation became acute after peace had been concluded with the foreign Powers, as it was time for the court to return to Peking. Preparations were being made for the journey when it became evident to those about him that the Emperor had not long to live. He became rapidly worse until there remained no possibility of moving him back to the capital.

Far from Peking, Jehol was the ideal spot for a conspiracy and a group of powerful nobles decided that after the death of the Emperor they would strike quickly and obtain the Regency by force for themselves. The leader of the conspiracy was Su Shun, an important minister who enjoyed the confidence of the Emperor, and this man intended to assume the supreme power and govern the country in the name of the five-year-old son of Yehonala. The plot included the imprisonment of Yehonala in the 'cold palace,' a place of punishment for disgraced concubines, the assassination of the Emperor's brothers and the massacre of all foreigners within the empire. In order to remove Yehonala from the scene, the Emperor was told of her alleged intimacy with Jung Lu, the young guards officer, and during the days when Hsien Feng lay dying the favourite concubine was kept from his chamber and remained in her own apartments in disgrace.

Li Lien-ying, the eunuch spy of Yehonala, acted as masseur to the Emperor, and in this capacity he was able to obtain information regarding the plans of the conspirators. He had been useful to his mistress on previous occasions, and now he was able to bring her sufficient details regarding her own danger to enable her to act. While outwardly she obeyed the orders of the Emperor, secretly she dispatched a message to Prince Kung, the Emperor's brother at Peking, requesting the immediate dispatch of troops of her own clan commanded by Jung Lu, her former lover and devoted friend. Her second step was to obtain the imperial seal without which no official decree was legal. The seal was stolen from the royal bed-chamber by her eunuch spy Li Lien-ying, and by the time that the Emperor had breathed his last, Jung Lu and the troops under his command had arrived.

Su Shun and the other nobles in the plot were forced to accompany the funeral cortège of the dead Emperor to Peking, but as the presence of the Empress and Yehonala was not required near the body, the ladies decided to hurry through the hills in order to reach the city before the funeral procession. The conspirators were aware of their intention and decided to have Yehonala murdered during the journey. Their attempt was frustrated by Jung Lu, who disobeyed orders and left his post beside the dead Emperor to gallop with his troops after the woman he loved. The story runs that he arrived outside her tent at the moment when an assassin was prepared to strike.

It was due to the assistance of this officer that Yehonala was able to reach the Forbidden City before her enemies, and once there she felt strong enough to take action against Su Shun and the other conspirators. Soon after their arrival with the body of the Emperor they were arrested. Su Shun was publicly decapitated and his immense wealth taken over by the Crown, while his associates were allowed to commit suicide. The especial severity shown towards Su Shun was thought to have been a revenge on the part of Yehonala for the many slights inflicted upon her by his wife during the days of her own disgrace at Jehol, when that lady had looked upon herself as a the future Empress and had treated Yehonala with the utmost contempt.

After the conspirators had been removed from the scene, the Empress-Consort and Yehonala were appointed joint regents for the young Emperor T'ung-chih, the son of Yehonala. The Empress-Consort was given the title of Tz'u An, meaning Motherly and Restful, while Yehonala became Tz'u Hsi, or Motherly and Auspicious. The former became Empress of the Eastern Palace and the latter of the Western. Jung Lu was appointed grand counsellor in recognition of his great services to the throne and was given one of the court ladies as his wife, a concession to public opinion on the part of the Empress Tz'u Hsi, as Yehonala was now called. There were to be no more rumours and no more scandal in regard to the relationship between the Empress and

her chosen adviser. She had learned her lesson at
Jehol.

Had the two Empress-Dowagers been equally ag-
gressive, and had each one been determined to have
her own way, such a solution would have proved to
be impossible, but fortunately for Tz'u Hsi her col-
league was content to be but the shadow and the
echo of the stronger woman. Only once during their
long association did she dare to assert her authority.
The supreme power was therefore concentrated in
the hands of the mother of the Emperor, and Tz'u
An remained but a figurehead as long as she lived.

Motherly and Auspicious was a strange title for a
young and beautiful woman of twenty-six, but it was
as the 'Benevolent Mother' that she was known to
the people of Peking, who referred to the 'Benign
Countenance' and considered her an example of
gentleness and mercy. Perhaps it was a desire to live
up to this ideal which made Tz'u Hsi identify herself
with the Buddhist goddess of Mercy, Kuan Yin, whom
she impersonated in plays and tableaux. Tz'u Hsi had
a passion for theatrical performances, but this particular pose may not have been all play-acting. Like
her great predecessor, the Empress Wu of the T'ang
dynasty, she must have eventually come to believe in
her own divinity after years of adulation and flattery.
The character of Tz'u Hsi was so complex that it
could include extremes. At one time she could be the
gentle mother, Kuan Yin, and at another the terrible
matriarch who ordered the favourite concubine of

an emperor to be thrown down a well as punishment for an indiscreet word. Tz'u Hsi was a woman of opposites. Good or bad, black or white, these were attributes which could be equally applied to her, but the shades of grey, the blending of black and white which form the essence of compromise, were also part of her nature. With her, the end always justified the means, and she was quite willing to use any methods which appeared to suit the situation.

Her treatment of Prince Kung, the brother of the late Emperor, during the early days of her Regency is typical of the domineering side of her nature. At first, when she was learning the art of government, Prince Kung, with his wide experience of state affairs, was appointed as 'adviser to the government,' while his daughter was adopted by the Empress and given the title of Princess Imperial. As time went on and Tz'u Hsi began to learn her way through the labyrinth of what we would call 'red tape,' the guidance which had first been welcome assumed the character of interference, and the relationship between the proud and independent sovereign and the equally proud and independent prince became strained. Good feeling was not aided by an attempt on the part of Prince Kung to encourage the Empress Tz'u An to take a more active part in the government. To appreciate the revenge of Tz'u Hsi it is necessary to make a mental picture of the scene.

The two Empresses were in the habit of holding joint audiences in the hall of the palace, each on her own throne, and each concealed by a yellow silk curtain from the ministers who were received. The advantage in this case was all with the ladies. While remaining completely hidden, they could still peep through the curtains and watch all that went on with an eye to any sign of disrespect or breach of etiquette. They were also able to remain comfortably seated while the ministers were obliged to kneel during the audience, a custom which had been originally instituted to protect the person of the Sovereign from a sudden attack. On one occasion, when Prince Kung ventured to rise from his knees too soon, Tz'u Hsi seized the opportunity for which she had been waiting. Calling out that she was being attacked, she ordered the guards to remove the unfortunate prince from the imperial presence. Her Majesty, in an edict, then stated that he was unworthy of her confidence and deprived him of all his offices.

In a month he was back in all his old posts except that of adviser to the government—perhaps because the official burial of the late Emperor was about to take place and Prince Kung had been in charge of preparing the tombs and providing the funds for the ceremonies. The body of Hsien Feng was buried with all pomp after four years of preparation, and according to custom, life-sized figures of concubines and eunuchs made of paper were placed beside him inside the tomb to act as his servants in the world of the spirits.

The most serious of the charges made against Tz'u

Hsi during the early years of her reign was her relationship with the eunuchs of the court. When K'ang
Hsi and Ch'ien Lung, the two most powerful
emperors of the Manchu dynasty, sat upon the throne,
their Majesties, who had studied the causes of the
fall of the Ming dynasty, took care that eunuchs
should be kept from all positions of authority. Their
movements were restricted to the capital, which they
were not allowed to leave. Later, under a succession
of weak monarchs, the eunuchs returned to power
to undermine and corrupt the imperial house as they
had previously undermined and corrupted the Ming
dynasty. Some of them amassed huge fortunes by
illegal means, and no purchase for the palace or for
the court was so small that some percentage of the
total amount did not find its way into their hands.

Tz'u Hsi was well aware of the evils of the system,
but being, in her own eyes at least, beyond the rules
which applied to others, she did not attempt to
destroy the power of the eunuchs, but used them for
her own ends. They were useful to her. Like her predecessor Wu Hou, she employed them as spies, and
she needed them for her amusements. Eventually she
saw her mistake, and her last words referred to the
undesirability of allowing eunuchs to meddle in the
government. But that was long after the days of
An-te-hai, the famous chief eunuch who was the
companion, one might almost say playmate, of the
young Empress.

An-te-hai was reported to be good-looking and he

was able to amuse Tz'u Hsi, two supremely important assets in the eyes of the Empress. Elaborate pageants and theatrical performances were arranged in which they both took part, and he accompanied his imperial mistress during excursions on the lake, both of them dressed in fancy costumes taken from historical plays. Many were the accusations levelled against this favourite, one of the most serious being that on occasions he wore the sacred Dragon robes, which only a sovereign was permitted to wear.

Rumour went so far as to report that An-te-hai was no eunuch but the father of a child born to Tz'u Hsi in the seclusion of the palace. The Empress was aware of these rumours and referred to them when she was an old woman, but at the time she took no steps to discredit the report. Such an eventuality would not have been without historical precedent, as the mother of the Emperor Shih Huang Ti, famous as the destroyer of the Confucian classics, had two children by a young man who was slipped into the palace and supposed to be a eunuch. The prominent position which An-te-hai enjoyed would have made such a supposition unlikely, but the rumour was given credence as it was known in every tea-house of Peking that An-te-hai's slightest wish was law in the Forbidden City.

Princess Der Ling, a lady-in-waiting to the Empress during the last years of her life, refutes this rumour and gives as its origin an even more fantastic tale. She says that the Empress-Dowager had two

panaceas for the preservation of youth and beauty.
The first was to eat ground-up pearls, and the second
to drink a little human milk every day. In order to
provide this strange form of adult nourishment,
various infants and their mothers were kept in the
palace, and it was one of these infants who was considered to be the child of the Empress. To the
Western mind the first tale sounds more plausible
than the second, but any explanation is possible when
applied to Tz'u Hsi.

The end of the favourite came suddenly. Dispatched
by the Empress to obtain funds for her private purse
in the south, he was forced to break the law of the
dynasty, which forbade a eunuch to leave the capital.
Once away from Peking, his arrogance and his orgies
caused such a scandal that a report of his conduct
reached the ears of Prince Kung. The Prince, who
had not forgotten his previous treatment at the hands
of the Empress when she had dismissed him from all
his offices, decided that the time had arrived for a
minor revenge, and he made up his mind to do away
with the chief eunuch. With this end in view he
approached the Empress-Dowager Tz'u An.

From all accounts the Empress Tz'u An was an
estimable woman. The son of Tz'u Hsi, the young
Emperor, was said to prefer her to his own mother,
and his successor on the throne also enjoyed her
society. Unfortunately, she lived in terror of her co-
regent, and this was the only occasion when she ever
dared to defy her openly. At the request of Prince

Kung she signed the decree authorizing the arrest and execution of the eunuch, and Tz'u Hsi was not informed of what had happened until after An-te-hai was dead. Tz'u Hsi was furious. Such a storm of rage burst forth in the palace that the Empress Tz'u An never dared to interfere again, and it is possible that she paid for this act of insubordination years later with her life.

The ugly eunuch, Li Lien-ying, who had stolen the imperial seal for his mistress at Jehol, was given the position of chief eunuch, but, wiser than his predecessor, he lived to possess a huge fortune and walk behind the body of the Empress when she was carried to her grave. As the evil genius behind the throne, his name has gone down to history coupled with that of the Empress-Dowager. The rôle which he played behind the scenes will never be entirely known, but Tz'u Hsi consulted him on all occasions, and his advice caused her to take many a false step. To give but one example: when money was needed to rebuild the Summer Palace, which had been destroyed by the foreign armies, Li suggested directing the funds destined for the navy to this purpose. The palace was rebuilt, but when war broke out with Japan there were neither ships nor supplies to meet the situation.

According to contemporary accounts, the eunuchs played an important part in debauching the son of Tz'u Hsi, the young Emperor T'ung-chih. Whether this was due to a deliberate policy on the part of his mother the Empress-Dowager is not known. She must have been aware of what was happening in the palace, and it may not have suited her policy to allow an undutiful and disrespectful son, so like herself in his arrogant nature, to attain supreme power. If T'ung-chih had been a strong ruler, her days of authority would have been over.

In November 1872 a decree was issued in the name of both Regents, transferring the duties of govern-ment to the young Emperor with many a pious wish for his future good behaviour, good wishes which were nipped in the bud by the eunuchs who en-couraged the young man in his evil ways. It was common knowledge that the Emperor frequented the worst resorts in the city under an assumed name, and that he was on intimate terms with the lowest of his subjects. Once he was recognized by an official of the court, who informed the authorities, and after this guards were appointed to follow him. The Emperor, far from being grateful, told the official at his next audience to mind his own business.

Trouble soon arose when the Emperor refused to submit state papers to his mother. In this attitude he was encouraged by his wife, A-lu-te, who urged her husband to assume a more independent attitude, not realizing the danger of opposing the autocratic Dowager. Like so many others who crossed the path of Tz'u, the unfortunate woman paid for her audacity with her own life and that of her unborn child.

Two years after his accession to the throne the Emperor contracted small-pox, an event which in

China is considered to be fortunate. The disease,
however, was too much for his health, undermined
as it was by dissipation, and on January 13th, 1875,
the Emperor 'ascended the Dragon' in the presence
of Prince Kung and his mother's friend, the inevitable Jung Lu. One can but wonder what were the
last thoughts of this young man, dying at the age of
nineteen under the watchful eye of the man who had
saved his mother, the Empress-Dowager, after the
death of her husband, and who had played such a
decisive rôle in establishing her on the throne. The
Emperor must have been aware of the intrigues
carried on inside the palace, and undoubtedly resented the influence of Jung Lu and his position of
power behind the throne.

The two Empress-Dowagers, with the usual show
of reluctance, resumed the Regency during the illness of T'ung-chih. Tz'u Hsi was firmly seated in the
saddle once more when the death of her son occurred,
and she acted at once. She called a grand council to
appoint a successor and at the same time took the
precaution of surrounding the palace with loyal
troops. A-lu-te, the wife of the dead Emperor, was
excluded from the council and left to weep over the
body of her husband. The ministers urged Tz'u Hsi
to keep the death of the Emperor a secret, and to
wait until after the birth of the child of A-lu-te to
name his successor, but the Empress-Dowager would
not hear of this. It was not part of her policy to allow
her son's wife to bear a son. If such an eventuality

occurred, A-lu-te would be Empress-Dowager and her own power, which had been founded on her position as Empress-mother, would be gone.

This was her last opportunity to retain the throne, and brushing aside the claims of A-lu-te, she chose the son of her brother-in-law, Prince Ch'un, who had married her own sister, as the successor to the dead Emperor. The ministers were against the choice but Tz'u Hsi, by virtue of her personality and determination, forced them to vote for her candidate. The boy was immediately sent for and brought to the palace at night, weeping bitterly. He was given the name of Kuang Hsu, meaning Glorious Succession, before he was turned over to the care of the eunuchs. A-lu-te, as an act of protest, and some say at the command of the Empress-Dowager, committed suicide.

Such were the events of that eventful night when Tz'u Hsi, for the second time in her career, struck before her life was over, because, having tasted power, she had no intention of letting it slip from her grasp. The secret of her choice was that the new boy Emperor was the son of her own sister. In her eyes he was a member of her own clan. Later she was to marry him to her niece in an attempt to divert the succession away from her husband's House. History was repeating itself. The ideals of the Empress Wu of the T'ang were again resurrected more than a thousand years after the death of the latter. But compromise was part of the complex nature of Tz'u Hsi, and she never resorted to the extreme methods used by her illustrious predecessors to secure the power for their own families. Perhaps because her whole heart was never in the attempt.

It is impossible not to refer to the sequel of this grim *coup d'état*, which is told by Princess Der Ling, the lady-in-waiting. It is the story of a plaster rabbit with a little red tongue. In her old age Her Majesty Tz'u Hsi, now affectionately called the Old Buddha, made a train journey to Mukden, where relics of the dead Emperors of the Manchu dynasty were preserved. Passing from the life-sized portrait of the Emperor Ch'ien Lung she came at last to a case containing the relics of her own son T'ung-chih, pitifully few in number as he had died so young. There under glass was his feeding-cup, the silver scales on which she had weighed his food, and his small yellow coronation robe embroidered with dragons. Two cases were filled with his toys and from one of these Tz'u Hsi took a white plaster rabbit which still shot forth a little red tongue and rolled its eyes. 'It was his favourite toy,' she said, taking it from the case. When she left the hall she was still holding it in her hand. 'The only time,' says the Princess Der Ling, 'that I ever saw her carry anything.'

The lady-in-waiting goes on to say, 'As Old Buddha looked at her son's relics, her heart in her face, I thought of what some historians had given to the world—that she had brought about her own son's death in order to become ruler of the Middle Kingdom—and wished that they might see her as I saw her. Mercifully, she never knew the story the world had been told.' But even the Princess Der Ling, who loved the Old Buddha, does not deny that she caused the death of A-lu-te, and the tiny ghost of an unborn child floats between our eyes and the sorrowing figure of the fierce old woman mourning over the toy of her lost son.

There are many stories told of the death of the co-regent Tz'u An, which took place shortly after the decease of the Emperor. The dark side of Tz'u Hsi's nature was more in evidence after the death of her son, and she had an old score to settle with Tz'u An, who had once openly opposed her. The new boy Emperor caused trouble between the two women. He made the mistake of taking his childish joys and sorrows to the Empress Tz'u An, instead of to his adopted mother, as Tz'u Hsi liked to be called, an insult which the latter was never able either to forget or forgive. She may have feared that eventually Tz'u An would become the power behind the throne if she continued to enjoy the affection of the young Emperor. But whatever the cause, Tz'u An died suddenly at the age of forty-six, after eating honey cakes, which some say were sent to her by her co-regent. Unfortunately her death did not remove the seeds of friction between the Empress-Dowager and her adopted son, which were already firmly planted in the ground, and which were to grow and ripen in the years to come and bring strife and bloodshed to the Middle Kingdom. As emperor he would have undoubtedly made mistakes, but the supreme mistake of his dynasty, that of the Boxer uprising, would never have taken place if he had been allowed to take an active part in the government.

It is rare that a dual personality is as obvious to the onlooker as it was in the case of Tz'u Hsi. The good and the bad not only warred within her, but in the world of reality good and bad influences stood in the flesh beside her, one on her right and one at her left hand. On the right was Jung Lu, her grand counsellor and devoted friend, a moderate and intelligent man with the welfare of the dynasty and that of his imperial mistress ever in his heart. He always made every effort first to prevent her follies, and later to save her from their consequences. On the left stood the eunuch Li Lien-ying, the humble cobbler of former days, ever ready with advice by which he could enrich himself or cause suffering to ·others. And because Tz'u Hsi trusted him implicitly, his position at court was unassailable. Men throughout the land walked in terror of this dark shadow, second only in power to the throne itself. He hated the new boy Emperor and bullied him during his childhood, and later many of the harsh measures taken against him were suggested by the eunuch. Li Lien-ying is responsible for the name of Old Buddha, which he gave to Tz'u Hsi and which she liked best of all her names. The Emperor, the young Empress-to-be, and even Jung Lu, were all secondary figures at court compared to Li Lien-ying.

When Kuang Hsu, the new Emperor, was seventeen years of age, the Empress-Dowager chose for him a wife from her own clan, the daughter of her brother. The Emperor disliked his cousin before he knew that she was destined to be his wife, but no power on earth could alter the choice of Tz'u Hsi once her own mind was made up. The young Empress was to be her super-spy, one who would always remain at the side of the Emperor and report his every move. It was not surprising, such being the case, that the affections of Kuang Hsu were centred on one of his secondary wives called the Pearl Concubine, an unfortunate woman who was later to incur the enmity of the Empress-Dowager. In spite of all the efforts of Tz'u Hsi, the relationship between the Emperor and his principal wife remained formal in the extreme. No child was ever born to them, and while every courtesy was shown to the young Empress in public, it was said that she was never called to her husband's private apartments. The Pearl Concubine shared his intimate life as well as his heart.

After the marriage of Kuang Hsu the time had once more arrived for the Empress-Dowager to step down from the throne and retire, as custom required, from active participation in the government. What better place could there be for her than the Summer Palace, just rebuilt with navy funds, and waiting, a joy to the eye and a delight to the senses, to receive her? Here she was to spend the next ten years among her flowers, taking excursions on the lake with her ladies and eunuchs, her houseboats threading in and out between masses of lotus buds. She had her beloved theatricals to amuse her, and plays were presented in a wonderful theatre of her own design with stages which could be moved up and down, while twelve imperial tailors designed costumes for her actors.

From the Summer Palace she could superintend all the activities that went on about her, from the rearing of silkworms to the breeding of Pekinese puppies. Flowers were her passion and we have a glimpse of her as a gardener, slipping out to cut or prune as her fancy dictated. 'It occurred to me,' wrote the Princess Der Ling, 'listening to her discourses on her court industries, that she would have been a marvellous business executive. Her ability to remember even the smallest detail was amazing.' Like Victoria of England, she was both 'narrowly domestic and widely imperial.'

The imperial side of her nature, although outwardly in abeyance, was, in actual practice, almost as active as it had been while she officially remained the head of the state. Audiences were held with the same regularity, and the Emperor was forced to make the long journey three times a week to the Summer Palace to pay his respects to the Old Buddha and consult with her on every subject of importance. He was never allowed to forget that the velvet glove which toyed with the lotus flower contained a mailed fist with a grip of iron. How he dared to plan his reforms and dream of opposing her we do not know, but dream and plan he did, and had he been but half as well served as his royal relative, his dreams might have come true. But it was his destiny to be betrayed, as it was hers to triumph, and the stars were against him from the beginning. The story of the attempt of Kuang Hsu to assert himself and throw off the all-enveloping tentacles of the Empress-Dowager is one of the strangest in history.

When all was ready for Kuang Hsu to launch his revolutionary reforms—of which the Empire stood badly in need—it occurred to this man, half dreamer and half plotter, that his powerful relative had best be kept out of the way. There is no record that he meant to harm her, he merely desired a cordon of troops thrown round the Summer Palace, and his intention was to keep her quietly at home until such time as his own plans should have matured. What he did feel it necessary to do was to order the assassination of Jung Lu, who stood in his way where the Old Buddha was concerned. Even an emperor could not swerve Jung Lu from his allegiance.

Unfortunately for Kuang Hsu, the man entrusted to carry out these orders was Yuan Shih-k'ai, who, instead of following instructions, went with all haste to Jung Lu, at Tientsin. Jung Lu was informed of a plot which included the assassination of the Empress-Dowager as well as of himself, and as he believed the story, he hastened back to Peking with Yuan Shih-k'ai and went direct to the Summer Palace. The Old Buddha struck, as was her habit, quickly. At three o'clock in the morning she started for the Forbidden City. The Emperor hurried to the gate to meet her, and flung himself on his knees. He knew when he heard she was on the way that all was lost.

All was lost as far as Kuang Hsu was concerned. He was to be the Old Buddha's prisoner as long as he lived, and for the next ten years follow her from one prison to another as she made her triumphant way from the Forbidden City to the Summer Palace and back again. Far better would it have been for him had she killed him on the spot, but that would not have suited her plans as she needed the figurehead of an Emperor, even if an impotent one, at the head of the state. The unhappy man passed the years writing in his diary and gazing across the lake from the small island where he was confined, separated from his beloved Pearl concubine, the only one on that dreadful day who had dared speak in his defence.

The end of the Pearl concubine was no less tragic. Until the time when the court fled from the foreign armies during the Boxer rebellion, she was imprisoned in the palace. Her food was of the coarsest and new garments were only given to her when the old ones fell from her in rags. In 1900, as the Old Buddha was about to leave for the interior of China, the Pearl was taken from her prison and thrown down a well by the eunuchs. Her only offence was that of faithfulness to her husband, the Emperor Kuang Hsu.

At the beginning of her third regency Tz'u Hsi was much annoyed by the sympathy shown the deposed

Emperor by the foreign legations and foreigners in general, both in China and abroad. Her hatred of the Westerners, if anything, increased, and she, as well as the majority of her subjects, attributed all their troubles to the presence of these unwanted visitors from abroad. The missionaries were especially disliked, because as their activities were not confined to the legation quarters, they travelled about the country more or less as they pleased.

As we have said before, the policy of Tz'u Hsi was to treat those whom she considered to be her inferiors as equals if their position was a strong one, and with this end in view she was in the habit of inviting the ladies of the foreign legations to tea. Some of these ladies, unfortunately, behaved in a manner not calculated to increase her respect for their countries: 'It was quite common for the foreign ladies to comment loudly upon the richness of dress of the court ladies and ladies-in-waiting, speculate on the probable price paid, and even to finger the rich materials, ignoring the wearers as of no account.' Curio hunting seems also to have been in vogue among the foreigners, and special court ladies were instructed to keep an eye on the gold and silver-ware during these visits, so that none of the pieces would be carried off as souvenirs.

All such incidents, petty as each one was in its own way, added fuel to the wrath of the Old Buddha, and when at length Prince Tuan showed her a forged dispatch reported to have come from the legations demanding her own abdication and the restoration of the Emperor, her fury broke forth. 'How dare they question my authority!' she exclaimed. 'The insults of these foreigners pass all bounds. Let us exterminate them before we eat our morning meal.'

Prince Tuan, the father of the boy whom Tz'u Hsi had appointed heir to the throne as an added insult to the deposed Emperor, was the power behind the Boxer movement. The Boxers themselves were mountebanks, strolling players or jugglers, travelling here and there over the Empire, giving performances by day and stealing what they could find at night. Their number was legion, and their ranks were recruited from the lowest dregs of the population. Prince Tuan, himself a degenerate and a renegade from his own class, had long associated himself with the Boxers and had learned their tricks and habits. In the beginning it had been his intention to wield them into an efficient fighting organization for his own amusement, but later he wished to use them as an instrument for driving the foreigners out of China. He hoped in this way to please the Old Buddha and retrieve for himself the prestige which his bad habits had caused him to lose. The movement was at the same time anti-foreign and anti-Christian. Although it began in a small way, it gathered momentum as time went on and grew with such speed that eventually it passed beyond the control of its organizers. Not only in Peking, but throughout the country, the Boxers terrorized the people on the slightest excuse, Chinese Christians as well as foreigners being especially singled out for persecution.

To give the Boxers additional driving force, Prince Tuan convinced them that they were invincible fighters and that no bullet or sword could slay them. This legend was universally believed by the common people, but the court was inclined to be sceptical and the Old Buddha herself had to be convinced before she would give the Boxers her unqualified support. For her benefit a performance was arranged in a courtyard of the palace. The Boxers crowded in, unwashed and unkempt, to the disgust of the court ladies, but the Old Buddha was impressed when two armed men attacked an unarmed Boxer and were unable to slay him. The onlookers realized that each move had been carefully rehearsed and that the whole exhibition was of an almost ritualistic character, but the Empress considered it a genuine test of the invulnerability of the Boxers themselves.

Jung Lu, with his sane and reasonable attitude, was against the Boxer movement from the beginning. His military experience made him realize that as troops they were not to be counted upon, and in any case China was in no position to fight the whole world. If the Old Buddha had listened to him there would have been no siege of the legations, no massacre of foreigners. When he refused to allow the heavy artillery, of which he was the custodian, to be used against the legations, he risked his position at court, and only his great influence with the Empress saved

his life when the Boxer leaders demanded his head
as the price of disobedience. His persistent efforts at
obstruction behind the scenes certainly saved the
legations from total destruction before relief arrived.

The Old Buddha has been blamed for the Boxer
movement and the terrible sufferings endured by the
inhabitants of the legations as well as by the Chinese
Christians during the long days of the siege. She gave
the order to start the bombardment, and only interfered with it when it suited her pleasure, such as on
the famous occasion when she ordered the guns to
cease firing during one of her picnics on the lake, as
they gave her a headache. But she was never consistent in her policy. Again two advisers were at her
elbow; Jung Lu, as before, on the right hand, but the
place on the left was now occupied by Prince Tuan,
although Li Lien-ying may have been behind him all
the while. Certainly a policy of destruction which
included marvellous opportunities for looting would
be dear to the heart of the eunuch, who no doubt
added to his already great fortune during this period
of unrest.

The actions of the Empress depended entirely upon
which adviser was in favour at the moment, and
which of the two policies she thought was likely to
win in the end. There were many times when Prince
Tuan was very much out of favour. At one time his
men were sent to search the palace itself for foreign
sympathizers and demanded the person of the
Emperor because of his previous interest in foreign

customs and ideas. Tz'u Hsi, furious at this intrusion on her privacy, left her bed at five o'clock in the morning to face a small army of armed and angry men. Her personal courage has never been questioned by either her friends or her enemies, and on this occasion, as on so many others, she dominated the situation through sheer force of personality. Her stinging words and haughty bearing caused confusion in the ranks of the Boxers. The reason for their visit was forgotten and they hastily left the Forbidden City in disorder.

Such a flagrant disregard of etiquette needed further punishment, and the Empress ordered the bombardment to cease. During the time that Prince Tuan remained in disgrace, daily presents of fruit, wine, vegetables, or ice were sent to the legations. But the day came when the star of Prince Tuan once more rose on the horizon. Then the bombardment was resumed, and a reward was offered for the head of any foreigner taken either dead or alive. Such rapid changes of policy puzzled the world, and they can only be accounted for by the presence of the good and the bad counsellor at the side of the Old Buddha. The see-saw of high politics went on while the legations suffered and wondered what forces were at work to cause such drastic changes of mood.

But in spite of her inconsistency, her poise remained with her to the end, and when flight had been decided upon, because the armies of the allies, on their way to relieve the legations, were sweeping towards Peking, it was the Old Buddha who saw to the hiding of her treasures and arranged the details of the journey. Dressed in cotton clothes, her hair done in a knot on top of her head, like any old peasant woman, she fled from the city with her prisoner the Emperor. They travelled in the two-wheeled carts used by the poor, and when, in four hours' time, they reached the Summer Palace, they were already covered with dust and in such a condition that the guards failed to recognize them. But the Old Buddha dared not linger, and with a hasty look at her beloved home she pushed on.

Some days later the travellers entered the district of Huai-lai, where they were greeted by the magistrate Wu Yung. This man was shocked at the condition in which he found the illustrious visitors. He writes that the Emperor 'was wearing a half-worn black silk wadded coat, wide in the skirt and sleeves, and he had no outside coat or waistcoat, nor had he a sash. His hair, where it should have been shaved, was an inch long, and his queue was disordered. His face was covered with dust, through which his skin showed yellow and dry.'

An interview took place between the magistrate and the Empress-Dowager, who was so pleased to see a faithful subject bowing down before her with proper respect, that the two wept together over the sad condition of the country. Then the Empress dried her tears and told him about their flight:

'Day by day we fled and had nothing to eat or drink. We were both cold and hungry. On the road we were thirsty. We told the eunuchs to get water. Though there were wells, there was either nothing with which to draw the water or else the wells would be filled with floating human heads. Unable to obtain water, they got me canes of giant millet which I chewed with the Emperor. . . . Last night the Emperor and I had only a bench between us, and we sat shoulder to shoulder watching the sky for morning. At daybreak the cold was intense and chilled us through. . . . Look at me! I am like an old country woman now. It is two days since we had food.'

Wu Yung, who after this time accompanied the court, records that 'on the seventeenth day of the eighth moon the travelling chariot arrived at Taiyuan' in the province of Shansi. Fortunately the governor's yamen, which was quickly converted into the 'travelling palace,' contained some fine curtains and hangings which had been made for an Emperor in the eighteenth century and which had never been used. These were now brought forth to provide a note of elegance to the provincial dwelling, and the court settled down to its usual routine as far as cramped quarters would permit. The young Empress, as well as certain ministers, eunuchs, and servants, had joined the party at different times on the route, all inadequately prepared for the journey and all in need of food. As the party increased in size the ingenuity of the local governors was taxed to provide such a large company with the necessities of life.

The heir to the throne, Prince Ta-Ah-Ko, the son of Prince Tuan, was not a welcome addition to the unhappy family party which surrounded the Old Buddha during the time of her exile. An official who wrote a detailed description of the court at this time says of him: 'He is fifteen years of age; fat, coarse-featured, and of rude manners. He favours military habits of deportment and dress, and to see him when he goes to the play, wearing a felt cap with gold braid, leather jerkins, and a red military overcoat, one would take him for a prize-fighter.' Prize-fighters and mountebanks were no longer the ideals of the Empress-Dowager, and she found it convenient upon her return to Peking to bow her head before the wishes of the allies and send Ta-Ah-Ko into exile with the others of his family. There was no longer any question of a son of Prince Tuan being allowed to sit upon the throne.

Exile for the Old Buddha was a time of anxious waiting. She followed with the greatest interest all the complicated negotiations of the peace treaty, and was ready to promise anything if only she could return to the capital and start to repair the havoc wrought by foreign troops to her beloved Summer Palace. It was a great relief to her when she heard of the final settlement, and the date of the departure of the court was fixed for the autumn of 1901.

The first part of the return journey was made by chair, as was customary, but now the court was accompanied by a large body of cavalry, as well as officials, eunuchs, and servants in great number. Much tribute from surrounding provinces had been sent to the Empress-Dowager in her exile, and three thousand carts were required to carry the baggage. On December 31st the party arrived at Cheng-tin-fu, where an epoch-making departure from precedent was about to take place. The court was to finish the journey by train. A delightful account of the great event was printed in the London *Times* during March 1902.

'The departure of the Court by a special train, long since prepared for its reception by the Belgian railway authorities and Sheng Hsuan-huai, was fixed for 9.30 a.m. in accordance with Her Majesty's orders; that Imperial and imperious lady, however, made her appearance at the station at seven o'clock, accompanied by the young Empress, the Imperial concubine, and the ladies-in-waiting. The Emperor had preceded her, and upon her arrival knelt on the platform to perform respectful obeisance, in the presence of an interested crowd. The next two hours were spent by the Empress, who showed no signs of fatigue, in supervision of the arrangements for dispatching the vast accumulation of her personal baggage, and in holding informal audiences with various high dignitaries, military and civil, on the platform.

'To the native spectators, the ladies of the Court with their eunuch attendants were as much objects of interest as the foreign railway officials; the Imperial concubine, "Chin" or "Lustrous" (sister of the unfortunate "Pearl"), a lively young person of pleasing appearance, attracting much attention. All the ladies of the Court wore pearls in profusion—those of the Empress being particularly fine—and all smoked cigarettes in place of the time-honoured waterpipe. During the Empress-Dowager's audiences, lasting sometimes over a quarter of an hour at a time, the Emperor stood close at her side; invariably silent, generally listless, though his expression when animated is described as conveying an impression of remarkable intelligence. The young Empress has good features, marred in European eyes by excessive use of paint; she, too, appeared to be melancholy, and showed but little interest in her surroundings. The Emperor and both Empresses were simply dressed in quiet coloured silks.

'The special carriages had been prepared at great expense under instructions issued by the Director-General of Railways. Those of the Empress-Dowager, the Emperor and his consort were luxuriously furnished with costly curios and upholstered in Imperial yellow silk; each had its throne, divan, and reception-room. Heavy window curtains had been thoughtfully provided in the carriages intended for the ladies' use; they were

not required, however, as none of the party showed
any desire for privacy during the entire journey.
While travelling, the carriage of the Empress-
Dowager was the general rendezvous of all the
ladies, attended by their eunuchs, the Empress-
Dowager spending much of the time in conversation with the Chief Eunuch—of somewhat notorious character—and the Emperor.

'It may be added, in conclusion, as a sign of the
times, that the Empress-Dowager's sleeping com-
partment was furnished with a European bed. It
contained also materials for opium smoking, of
luxurious yet workmanlike appearance.'

If the entire court was obliged to stand during the
journey, as is reported to have been the case on
another occasion, we might wonder if the ladies
found the journey as agreeable as did the Empress
with her throne and European bed.

It is interesting to speculate whether or not the
Old Buddha ever realized how close she and all her
dynasty had been to complete disaster. Certainly she
gave no indication of having such knowledge when
she resumed her life in the Forbidden City. Repairs
were quickly made, and the Summer Palace soon
showed no signs of an alien occupation, except for
certain marks on the stones which were allowed to
remain to remind her that foreign guns had once been
there. They were left so that she would bever forget
her greatest mistake.

Life at court resumed its accustomed round with the usual theatricals, and tea parties were again given for the ladies of the legations. Foreign ministers were received at court as if nothing at all had happened, and people began to wonder if anything indeed had happened in which the Old Buddha had played a part. The Boxer leaders were punished and were either killed or went into exile, and soon Jung Lu was to disappear from her life as well, but not before his daughter had been married to Prince Ch'un and had given birth to another boy-emperor called to the throne by Tz'u Hsi. This boy was called Pu Yi and was destined to be the last Manchu Emperor to sit upon the throne of China.

It was a sad day for Tz'u Hsi when word was brought of the death of Jung Lu. There were more lines in her face after that and people who knew her said that she was never quite the same again. He had held the two highest posts open to a subject in China, namely, the position of Grand-Secretary and of Grand-Counsellor. When he died at the age of sixty-seven he was given the posthumous designation of 'Learned and Loyal.' Her Majesty paid the funeral expenses herself, and in a decree issued soon after his death, said: 'He (Jung Lu) was absolutely indispensable to us and we depended entirely upon his advice.'

The Old Buddha was getting old, and perhaps she was lonely after the death of Jung Lu. Hate is a poor companion for old age, and hate seems to have been the dominant emotion in the palace. The Old Buddha hated her prisoner the Emperor with a hatred that burned fierce and bright throughout the years, and which he returned in full measure. Kuang Hsu hated the young Empress his wife, as well as his concubine 'Lustrous,' who reminded him of her dead sister 'The Pearl.' But all these little private hates were as nothing compared to the universal hymn of hate directed towards the eunuch Li Lien-ying, the arch-fiend of the palace.

For fifty years the Old Buddha had sat in lonely state on the throne of China, and the magnificence must have begun to pall, and even the beloved theatricals to lose their charm. She must have suffered greatly as she agreed to all the reforms that Kuang Hsu had been so ready to give the Empire during his brief span of power. There was little enough left except the empty show of power to sweeten her last years. Her wings were clipped and Jung Lu was no longer there to help her meet the new age. In 1907 she had a slight stroke, and then she must have realized that she had not much longer to live. Perhaps the anger and rage against the foreigners had eaten into her soul until a new victim was demanded, if only to prove to herself that she was not a frustrated old woman. The easiest and most obvious victim was the Emperor Kuang Hsu.

No one knows exactly how he died. Li Lien-ying watched over him until the end and he is said to have administered slow poison at the Empress's orders.

312

The eunuch himself had plenty of reasons to wish the Emperor out of the way. He must have shared the general conviction that the Old Buddha's days were numbered and realized that she was his only protector at court. For years he had tormented the Emperor and knew that he had nothing to expect except death by the 'slow slicing process' if Kuang Hsu resumed the throne. But whether by order of the Empress-Dowager, or solely through the initiative of Li Lien-ying, word went forth that the Emperor was about to die, and long before Kuang Hsu turned his face to the wall and breathed his last, the eunuchs were busily engaged in preparing his grave clothes.

With the Emperor safely out of the way, the boy Pu Yi was brought to the palace and crowned, very much as his predecessor had been brought, weeping and at night. The Old Buddha had her way until the end, but after the coronation and a long and exciting day, she was stricken in her turn. During her last hours her voice remained clear and calm as she dictated her decrees nominating Prince Ch'un as Regent, and arranged that her niece, the young Empress, should have her reward: a share of the power. She was as calm as if she were about to set out once more for the Summer Palace, instead of on that last journey from which there would be no return. Her last words of advice were strange ones to be uttered by a woman who for fifty years had held the state in the hollow of her hand:

'Never again,' said the Old Buddha to those gathered about her bedside, 'allow any woman to hold the supreme power in the state. It is against the house-law of our Dynasty and should be strictly forbidden.'

So passed the Old Buddha, supreme autocrat but very much a woman to the end. Above all laws in her own eyes, she caused others to see her in the same light, and to think of her as one above good and evil. Three years later the dynasty came to an end, slipping through the fingers of the boy Pu Yi, and with its crash came chaos to the Chinese people. The Republic with all its accompanying miseries has held the stage for the past quarter of a century, but what is a quarter of a century in the long history of Chinese civilization? Events move more rapidly today than ever before, and who knows but that we or our children may yet see another emperor on the throne of China, the Summer Palace once more restored to its former brilliance, and the curtain rung up on the next act of the great drama of imperial court life.

SOURCES

SOURCES

I

Wives, Concubines and Courtesans

PAGE

23. *Beyond the Wei.* Legge i., vol. iv, p. 148.
24. *If you, Sir, think kindly of me.* Legge i., vol. iv, p. 140.
24. *I pray you, Mr. Chung.* Legge i, vol. iv, p. 126.
26. *At fourteen I married my Lord you.* Poem by Li T'ai-po. Rendered into English by Ezra Pound.
27. *At fifteen I stopped scowling.* Poem by Li T'ai-po. Rendered into English by Ezra Pound.
27. *It is more meritorious.* H. G. Creel, 'The Birth of China.'
30. *In every nation the happiness of women.* Lin Yutang, 'My Country and My People.'
31. *Women are more deadly to scholars.* Younghill Kang, 'The Grass Roof.'
33. *Pray who in the glorious Han Palaces.* Poem by Li T'ai-po. Rendered into English by H. W. Houlding.
35. *Sun Shou had a good complexion.* Translated by Professor W. P. Yetts from the History of the Later Han.
35. *Description of Han beauties.* From a lecture by Professor W. P. Yetts.
39. *I have your letter.* J. O. P. Bland and E. Backhouse, 'Annals and Memoirs of the Court at Peking.'
40. *The Heir Apparent is safely ensconced.* J. O. P. Bland and E. Backhouse, 'Annals and Memoirs of the Court at Peking.'
42. *Rare are they.* H. A. Giles, 'Gems of Chinese Literature.'

II

The Most Beautiful of Chinese Women

SOURCES

III

A Despotic Empress

PAGE
72. *When a country is about to collapse.* Parker, 'Ancient China Simplified.'
76. *When in the service of the late King.* H. A. Giles, 'Chinese Biographical Dictionary.'
79. *When the House of Han arose.* H. A. Giles, 'Chinese Literature.'
82. *The Emperor Kao.* H. A. Giles, 'Chinese Literature.'
83. *If I, with only a linen garment.* L. Wieger, 'Textes Historiques,' vol. i.
85. *This is not the work of a human being.* L. Wieger, 'Textes Historiques,' vol. i.
87. *Oh, my friend.* H. A. Giles, 'Chinese Literature.'
88. *'These barbarians are beasts.'* Parker, 'A Thousand Years of the Tartars.'
89. *What need have I of your book.* L. Wieger, 'Textes Historiques,' vol. i.

IV

A Feminist of Long Ago

95. *Honour and dishonour, poverty and wealth.* The quotations in this chapter from 'Pan Chao,' by Miss Nancy Lee Swann, are reprinted with the kind permission of the American Historical Society and the D. Appleton-Century Co. of New York City.
98. *When the concubine Pan.* L. Binyon, Monograph on the Ku K'ai-Chih scroll.

SOURCES

V

Princesses in Exile

117. *Moon over the houses of Han, over the site of Ch'in.* F. Ayscough, 'Fur Flower Tablets.' By kind permission of Messrs. Houghton Mifflin and Co., Boston, Mass.
118. *She did not speak loudly.* F. Ayscough, 'Fur Flower Tablets.' By kind permission of Messrs. Houghton Mifflin and Co., Boston, Mass.
123. *'Their custom,'* he said. E. H. Parker, 'A Thousand Years of the Tartars.'
123. *Ever since the hour of my surrender.* H. A. Giles, 'Chinese Literature.'
124. *'Why not,'* he said. L. Wieger, 'Textes Historique,' vol. i.
125. *I propose to have a frontier trade.* E. H. Parker, 'A Thousand Years of the Tartars.'
131. *To be free from jealousy.* Charles Bell, 'The People of Tibet.'
133. *She was a maiden of seventeen.* Colonel Henry Yule, 'The Book of Ser Marco Polo.'

VI

The Empress Wu

141. *The Emperor T'ai Tsung.* H. A. Giles, 'Gems of Chinese Literature.'
146. *Although I never shared the bed.* Amyiot, 'Les Mémoires concernant les Chinois,' vol. v.
149. *If your Majesty.* Amyiot, 'Les Mémoires concernant les Chinois,' Vol. V.

321   X

VII

The Beloved of an Emperor

SOURCES

PAGE

190. *Pray who in the glorious Han Palaces.*   From a poem by Li
     T'ai-po, translated by H. W. Houlding.
191. *Wu Tao-tzu, the darling of his age.*   L. Binyon, 'Chinese
     Painting.'
192. *Towards the pavilion of porcelain.*   From a poem by Tu Fu,
     rendered into English by E. Powys Mathers.
193. *The Unworthy One has been intractable.*   F. Ayscough, 'Tu
     Fu.'
194. *Not one but feared that propriety.*   F. Ayscough, 'Tu Fu.'
197. *If Tu Fu had said that Yang Kuei-fei.*   F. Ayscough, 'Tu
     Fu.'
199. *My heart recalls our escape at the beginning of the rebellion.*
     F. Ayscough, 'Tu Fu.'
201. *At this moment Imperial consorts, ladies of lesser rank are
     massacred.*   F. Ayscough, 'Tu Fu.'
201. *Now all below the sky falls in ruins.*   F. Ayscough, 'Tu Fu.'
204. *The son used a great knife.*   F. Ayscough, 'Tu Fu.'
205. *Remembering the stories told of her.*   From 'The Orchid
     Door,' a collection of ancient Korean poems
     rendered into English by Joan S. Grigsby.

VIII

A Taoist Nun

209. *A Taoist Nun.*   The principal events of the life of Yu
     Hsuan-chi are taken from 'Selling Wilted Peonies,'
     by Genieve Wimsatt.
211. *I humbly pray.*   H. A. Giles, 'Gems of Chinese
     Literature.'
211. *Achieve the supreme.*   G. Wimsatt, 'Selling Wilted
     Peonies.'

IX

Precious Pearl

X

The Perfumed Princess

XI

The Last Great Ruler of China

INDEX

INDEX

INDEX

INDEX

Po P'i, Prime Minister of the State of Wu, 56, 61
Precious Pearl, Ming Empress, 231–250; her father, 235; chosen empress, 237; her enemies, 240; death of the emperor, 247; commits suicide, 249
Pu Yi, Last Manchu Emperor, 311, 314

Round Faced Beauty, 37–40

Shih Huang Ti, First Emperor of China, 69–72, 287
Shou, T'ang Prince, 180
Shu-Sen T'ung, Confucian Scholar, 80
Song-tsen Gam-po, King of Tibet, 127–131
Ssu-ma Ch'ien, the Historian, 74, 79, 104
Su-Shun, Manchu Minister, 280–282
Sun Shou, Han Beauty, 33, 34

Ta-Ah-Ko, Manchu Prince, 301, 307
Tale of Gengi, 183–184
T'ang T'ai Tsung, T'ang Emperor, *see* Li Shih-min
Taoist Mysteries, 181, 191, 209–212
Tartars, 125, 126, 144, 196
Teng, Han Empress, 109
Tibet, Tibetans, 127–132
Tu Fu, 155, 175, 186, 187, 189, 196–197, 200–201, 204, 212
Tuan, Manchu Prince, 300–304, 307
T'ung-chih, Manchu Emperor, 282, 289–291, 293

Tz'u An, Manchu Empress, 276, 282, 284, 288, 294
Tz'u Hsi, Manchu Empress-Dowager, 14, 90, 92, 271–314; birth, 275; becomes an imperial concubine, 276; overthrows a conspiracy, 282; regent of the empire, 282; places her candidate on the throne, 292; "Old Buddha," 295; flight, 305; return to Peking, 310; death, 313

Wei Chung-hsien, a Eunuch, 233, 237–246
Wen, Ancient King of China, 94
Wen Chung, Prime Minister of Yueh, 47
Wen Fei ch'ing, the Flying Minister, 220–225
Wen-ch'eng, T'ang Princess, 127–132
Wu Chao, *see* Wu Hou
Wu, Han Emperor, 33
Wu Hou, T'ang Empress, 90, 137–171; imperial concubine for the first time, 140; second time, 144; proclaimed empress, 150; worships the powers of heaven, 157; recalls her son to the throne, 167; deposed, 170, 283, 286, 292
Wu San Kuei, Ming General, 37–40, 249
Wu Tao-tzu, Chinese Painter, 191
Wu Tsung, T'ang Emperor, 209
Wu Yung, Manchu Magistrate, 305–306

Yang Ch'in Kuo, Sister of Yang Kuei-fei, 184
Yang Han Kuo, Sister of Yang Kuei-fei, 184

331

INDEX